HAPPY FATHER'S DAY!

Love,

your kids...

INTRODUCTION TO THE

DECORATIVE A·R·T·S

1890 TO THE PRESENT DAY

INTRODUCTION TO THE

DECORATIVE A·R·T·S

1890 TO THE PRESENT DAY

EDITED BY AMANDA O'NEILL

TIGER BOOKS INTERNATIONAL
LONDON

A QUINTET BOOK

This edition first published 1990 by
Tiger Books International PLC

Copyright © 1990 Quintet Publishing Limited.
ISBN 1-85501-053-4

This book was designed and produced by
Quintet Publishing Limited
6 Blundell Street
London N7 9BH

Creative Director: Peter Bridgewater
Designer: Neal Cobourne
Project Editor: Amanda O'Neill
Editor: Lindsay Porter

Typeset in Great Britain by
Central Southern Typesetters, Eastbourne
Manufactured in Hong Kong by
Regent Publishing Services Limited
Printed in Hong Kong by
Leefung-Asco Printers Limited

CONtents

INTRO*duction*

THE LAST YEARS OF THE NINETEENTH CENTURY HERALDED THE ONSET OF THE MODERN AGE. THE INDUSTRIAL REVOLUTION RUMbled on; electricity and photography were nascent sciences; innovative technologies were bursting upon an advancing Western world – and the first fine art to be called 'modern' (by later art historians) was being created by Manet, Cézanne, Monet and their contemporaries.

In the decorative arts, too, signs of a new age were beginning to reveal themselves, in techniques, materials, themes, influences and purpose. From now on a series of exciting new movements was to arise from the interaction between the past and this new industrial era, sometimes reacting against and sometimes revelling in the machine age. This book takes a broad look at the four major movements – Arts and Crafts, Art Nouveau, Art Deco and Modernism – and the subsequent developments in the decorative arts from 1890 to the present day. It is of necessity simplified, because although each of the movements is distinct and distinguishable from the others in itself, the divisions between them are far from being as clear-cut as the chapter headings imply. The phases of transition from one style to another were often subtle and fluid, and indeed the classification of a particular designer or piece of design under one heading or another may be arguable – one author's Modernism can easily become another's Art Deco.

At the outset of our period, the Arts and Crafts Movement (1850–1920) was still a force to be reckoned with. It is generally considered as a movement which looked back, rather than ahead, for its inspiration and guiding principles. The movement, whose leading exponents were the critic John Ruskin and the multi-talented designer-writer William Morris, was essentially a reaction against the encroaching modern age. Arts and Crafts designs signalled a romantic, though not rigid, return to earlier, purer aesthetics and techniques; their creators took their inspiration largely from what they viewed as the simple, unsullied Middle Ages – its cathedrals, furnishings, even costumes, and perhaps most significantly, its workers' guilds and their rules and methods.

As the part played by the Arts and Crafts Movement decreased, Art Nouveau (1890–1910) began to emerge with all its waves and tendrils, *femmes fatales* and comely maidens, botanical verity and Symbolist allusions. There was the hyper-organic furniture and ironwork of Hector Guimard, the botanically inspired glass and wood of Emile Gallé and Louis Majorelle, but most of all the exquisitely crafted, often dazzlingly pictorial goldsmith's work of René Lalique, Georges Fouquet and other Parisian jewellers. Unlike Arts and Crafts designers, its adherents rejected the examples of antiquity and sought to create a new and modern design vocabulary.

Art Nouveau, however, was a style with no logical route for development and growth, and as its popularity waned, designers sought a new direction. The 1920s and 1930s were the era of the flapper, the Jazz Age, the Machine Age, the between-the-wars decades: carefree

RIGHT *A Daum vase*

CENTRE *Chair by Mies van der Rohe, c 1929*

BELOW RIGHT *'Space Walk' by Sue Thatcher, 1960s*

BELOW *Dragonfly corsage ornament by René Lalique*

BELOW LEFT *'Medway' printed cotton by William Morris*

and conservative in equal measures. The artistic output of the period reflected this variety. At the International Exhibition of Decorative and Industrial Arts held in Paris during the summer of 1925 the new style – or rather styles – emerged. These included high-style Art Deco and the more functional form known as *Moderne*, which was to slide imperceptibly into Modernism.

Art Deco has been described as the last total style, the last movement to pervade all areas of the decorative arts across Europe and the United States. Its refined elegance was to give way to the new doctrines of functionalism, symbolized by machines and especially automobiles. New and revolutionary steel furniture began to appear from the Bauhaus in Germany. The elegance of Art Deco was replaced by the hard chic of steel and angular, unadorned surfaces. The conviction that design should be determined by need and function, and at the same time achieve a 'state of platonic grandeur [and] mathematical order' was fundamental to Modernist theory during the 1920s and 1930s.

After World War II, there were to be no more 'total' movements; yet few periods in the history of the decorative arts have been as rich and complex as the postwar years. Design revolutions in all fields, from furniture to ceramics, from photography to jewellery, have been taking place; social, technological and economic changes, as well as developing aesthetic changes, have all played their part in forming the shape of the applied arts of the era. The introduction of cheap reproduction processes, often involving the use of plastic, has brought 'good' design within the reach of a wide public. At the same time, the exclusive interior designer has remained a powerful figure, producing expensive and finely-made artefacts for a wealthy clientele. The influence of the great classics of Modernism – the furniture and objects created by such masters as Mies van der Rohe and Le Corbusier – has grown during the postwar period, but other tendencies have also helped to shape contemporary design: Pop Art and pop culture, nostalgia and revivalism. Innovation and growth continue to be apparent in the decorative arts today.

1. ARTS *& crafts*

LEFT *Morris and Company embroidered screen, probably designed by May Morris for the drawing room of Bullerswood, the home of the Sanderson family, about 1889.*

THE ARTS AND CRAFTS MOVEMENT DEVELOPED IN ENGLAND DURING THE SECOND HALF OF THE NINETEENTH CENTURY AS A PROTEST against the character of mid-Victorian manufactured products. It incorporated a variety of artists, writers and craftsmen so wide that it is difficult to define the limits of the movement. Some of its precursors were deeply conservative and looked wistfully back to a medieval past, while others were socialists and reformers. Some, like John Ruskin (1819–1900), identified the Arts and Crafts aesthetic with Protestantism, while others, such as the architect Augustus Welby Pugin (1812–52), saw a clear affinity between the revival of medievalism and the Catholic cause. Some members of the movement, such as the designers William Morris (1834–96) and C. R. Ashbee (1863–1942) cherished handicraft and tended to reject the opportunity to produce for a mass market. Others, such as the architect Frank Lloyd Wright (1867–1959), positively relished the creative and social advantages of machine production.

The unifying factor within the movement was the belief that mid-nineteenth-century design had gone astray. Its members not only condemned the shoddy workmanship, indiscriminate use of materials, inefficient forms and elaborate ornamentation that characterized most mid-Victorian manufactured products, but believed that such products had a deleterious effect upon society. The idea that a well-designed environment – fashioned with beautiful and well-crafted buildings, furniture, tapestries and ceramics – would improve the fabric of society was expressed by William Morris in the middle of the nineteenth century and repeated constantly thereafter. To achieve this goal, those involved sought to restore pride in craftsmanship rather than soulless mechanical production. They strove therefore to ensure that traditional methods of handcraftsmanship would survive, despite competition with machine production; to ameliorate the working conditions of artisans and craftsmen, and to encourage artistic collaboration amongst workers. Their intention was to improve the quality of life for everyone by restoring integrity to the objects common to daily living.

RIGHT *For Morris, tapestry constituted 'the noblest of the weaving arts'. In 1879 he set up his first experimental loom at Kelmscott House, where he taught himself to weave with the help of eighteenth-century French manuals. In 1881 he and his apprentice, J. H. Dearle, who was to become one of the firm's leading designers, set up production on a large scale at Merton Abbey. 'The Orchard tapestry' woven at Merton in 1890 for Jesus College Chapel, Cambridge, is an example of their use of the high-warp, or vertical, tapestry technique.*

Frederick Allen Whiting, a Boston design reformer, described the erosion of individuality in traditional crafts such as chair-making. At one time, he wrote 'every chair was lovingly wrought out by hand by a man who was interested in his work for its own sake [who] believed that everything has an inherent beauty which it is the craftsman's duty and privilege to bring forth, and who defends, because of the power of expression it gave him, his craft with his skill of workmanship . . . A chair made under such circumstances and traditions, by such a craftsman', Whiting continued, 'was fit for two centuries of use, and bore in its every line and part, evidence of human thought and feeling.'

Arts and Crafts designers held an ideal of furniture made 'for beauty's sake' as much as for use. (Below) Morris's bed at Kelmscott Manor, with hangings and cover designed by May Morris about 1893. The cover was embroidered by Jane Morris, while the hangings were worked by May, assisted by Lily Yeats (sister of the poet) and Ellen Wright. The verse is by Morris. (below right) Washstand, in painted and gilt wood, by William Burgess, for his own house, Tower House, London, about 1880. This washstand, which is inscribed Venez Lavez, *is typical of Burgess's flamboyant interpretation of medieval precedents.*

By contrast, in his day, Whiting stated, 'we now have a very different picture – that of the manager in his office who receives an order for 100 of No. 674, which he passes on to the foreman who distributes the orders to John for the legs, to Silas for the backs, to William for the frames, and so on . . . each man turning out the [given part] on his special machine. Then the different pieces are sent to the assembling rooms to be put together by 'specialists' whence they move on again to still others who sandpaper, putty, scrape or fill, varnish or polish. The completed chairs – 100 or 1,000 of them – are as identical and as perfect as accurate machinery can make them, but with hardly a touch of human interest left by one of the many hands through which they have passed.'

Reformers like Whiting hoped to improve design by returning to conditions they believed had been typical before the Industrial Revolution. By replacing the limited perspective of the machine operator working in relative isolation with the comprehensive vision of the craftsman, they aimed to restore dignity to the maker, integrity to the product, discrimination to the user and artistic cooperation throughout the design process.

Although the questionable standards of mid-Victorian manufactured products undoubtedly justified the need for reform, the ideals of English design reformers would never have gained international acceptance without the benefits of a strong and widely publicized philosophical argument. This was propounded chiefly by three ardent advocates, AWN Pugin, John Ruskin and William Morris who, by word and deed, spread the message not only within Britain, but throughout the industrialized world.

The design reformer's major premise, that the character of the living and working environment moulds the character of the individual, evolved from a related idea promulgated by Pugin in the 1830s. A designer, writer and the son of a French emigré architect, Pugin believed that the character of a nation was expressed through its architecture and applied arts. He recommended that English architects and designers should abandon their allegiance to Graeco-Roman models in favour of Gothic examples from the late Middle Ages, the greater suitability of the latter, he argued, stemming from its association with a Christian rather than a pagan culture. He made this case passionately in such books as *Contrasts* and *The True Principles of Pointed or Christian Architecture*.

Pugin distinguished himself from many other Gothic revivalists by equating the appearance of medieval buildings with the spiritual refinement of the Middle Ages. The Gothic had long been employed either for its picturesque characteristics or as a nationalistic antidote to the international classical style. Pugin, however, maintained that Gothic was less a style than an architectural representation of Christian sentiment, and spiritually vacuous building of his own age.

In addition to their symbolic appropriateness, Pugin maintained that Gothic and other styles from the Middle Ages were superior for their integrity. He admired the functional nature of the plan, the expressive quality of the façade and the integration of structure and ornament that characterized medieval architecture. He suggested that such features were absent from contemporary British architecture and he recommended that architects and designers could learn valuable lessons by studying the work of their medieval predecessors. 'There should be no features about a building which are not necessary for convenience, construction or propriety.'

With a similarly pragmatic attitude, he stated: 'all ornaments should consist of enrichment of the essential construction of the building', advocating a degree of decorative restraint.

His belief in the moral and aesthetic superiority of the Gothic style inspired a generation of architects and designers (many of whom trained supporters of the Arts and Crafts Movement) and stimulated enthusiasm for the Gothic Revival style in Britain and abroad.

Like Pugin, John Ruskin, architectural critic and first Slade Professor at Oxford (1868), equated the character of the nation with that of its architecture. He believed that the nature of contemporary British architecture would improve if it were designed to express qualities exemplified by the Romanesque and Gothic styles. In the *Seven Lamps of Architecture* (1849), he identified those qualities as Sacrifice, Truth, Power, Beauty, Life, Memory and Obedience, and explained how each might be conveyed by form, ornament or construction. He also

addressed the issue of construction, demonstrating that he was as concerned with the process of building as with the finished product. He suggested that architecture must reflect the thoughtfulness and feeling of each individual involved in its construction. 'I believe the right question to ask, respecting all ornament,' he wrote in *The Lamp of Life*, is simply this: Was it done with enjoyment . . ., was the carver happy while he was about it?

Ruskin continued to explore this theme in *The Stones of Venice* (1851–53), an influential work in three volumes that provided an indepth analysis of Venetian architecture from the Middle Ages. In one section, an essay entitled 'On the Nature of Gothic', Ruskin summarized the qualities that gave medieval architecture its distinctive character. These included Rudeness (imperfection or lack of precision), Changefulness (variety, asymmetry, and random placement of elements), Naturalism (truthfulness or realism as opposed to conventionalization), Grotesqueness (delight in the fantastic). Rigidity (conveyed by sprightly or energetic forms and ornament), and lastly Redundance (achieved through the repetition of ornament). He viewed each quality as an extension of the craftsman's personality, and each was essential to achieving an architecture of character.

As long as the 'division of labour' degraded the 'operative [or worker] into a machine,' architecture would fail to achieve the qualities of medieval architects. He advocated changing the design process to foster an environment of 'healthy and ennobling labour.' To achieve such an atmosphere, he proposed 'three broad and simple rules' to be applied by architects, designers and manufacturers: '1. Never encourage the manufacture of an article not absolutely necessary, in the production of which Invention has no share. 2. Never demand an exact finish for its own sake, but only for some practical or noble end. 3. Never encourage imitation or copying of any kind, except for the sake of preserving records of great works.' Without dictating a specific formula for design reform, Ruskin established an ideal; and for the next 70 years, that ideal, as set forth in 'On the Nature of Gothic', continued to inspire reformers.

The leader of the reform movement was William Morris. As a student, Morris developed a profound affection for the culture of the Middle Ages. His sensitivity to his surroundings was strengthened by a two-year apprenticeship in the Oxford office of the Gothic Revival architect, George Edmund Street. Although he abandoned architecture to take up painting, the time Morris spent in Street's office was invaluable, for it was there that he developed a lifelong friendship with the senior clerk, Philip Webb whom he had met at Oxford.

This friendship was one of several fortuitous connections made by Morris at Oxford. While there, he also met a fellow painter, Edward Burne-Jones, who became his room-mate and travelling companion, and still another painter and poet, Dante Gabriel Rossetti, both of whom, with him, were later to be members of the Pre-Raphaelite Brotherhood. Like Webb, they shared Morris's passion for the culture of the Middle Ages. They were inspired not only by its architecture, art and craft, but also by the artistic cooperation which had fostered their creation.

The commitment of these friends to the artisanry and atmosphere of the Middle Ages was tangibly expressed in Red House, the marital home designed by Webb for Morris and his bride, Jane Burden. The house is as significant for the manner in which it was built and furnished as for its warm and unassuming appearance. Proudly handcrafted by workers involved throughout the building process, it was in essence a communal labour of love to which Morris's entire circle of artistic friends contributed. A unified whole, related from large-scale to small, from site to hardware, and from exterior to interior, it has become a monument of the Arts and Crafts Movement, not so much for what it is, but for what it symbolizes.

The collaborative effort manifest in Red House prompted the formation in 1861 of Morris, Marshall, Faulkner & Co. 'Fine Art Workmen in Painting, Carving, Furniture and the Metals.' The company was of unparalleled importance in the Arts and Crafts Movement and established theoretical and practical precedents followed by similar communities in

ABOVE *Majolica plate designed by Pugin, c 1850.*

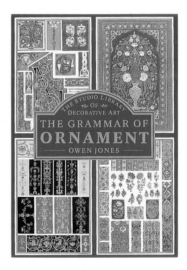

LEFT *Owen Jones's* The Grammar of Ornament, *published in 1856, set out a wide selection of historical styles of decoration ranging from ancient Greek and Celtic to Louis Quinze and late Stuart. Its fine chromolithographic plates were a source of inspiration to many Arts and Crafts designers.*

Europe and the United States. The beginnings of Morris, Marshall, Faulkner and Co., however, were rather uncertain. Rossetti one of the founder members of the firm, recounted some years later that the idea of this business venture began as little more than a joke. A discussion began among some of the painters and architects who had designed and decorated the Red House regarding the way in which artists of the Middle Ages undertook not only painting and sculpture but also many other *métiers*. A small sum of money was raised as capital and Rossetti, Madox Brown, Burne-Jones, Webb, P. P. Marshall, C. J. Faulkner and Morris decided to establish their own community of 'fine art workmen'. The firm's prospectus declared its intentions. Diversely working in stained glass, mural decoration, carving, metalwork, furniture and embroidery, Morris, Marshall, Faulkner and Co. lent its weight to the reform of the decorative arts in England.

Morris described decorative art historically as a natural form of human feeling and expression, as an 'art of the unconscious intelligence'.

'Everything', he wrote, 'made by man's hand has a form which must be either beautiful or ugly.' If the craftsman or woman follows the example of nature on his or her design, the result, Morris maintained, will necessarily be beautiful. If nature's example is ignored, the product will turn out to be ugly. Morris neatly described beautiful decoration as an 'alliance with nature.' The craftsman or woman must work in the way that nature does 'till the web, the cup or the knife, look as natural, nay as lovely, as the green field, the river bank, or the mountain flint.'

The decorative arts had a formidable opponent in the philistinism of the Victorian middle classes. Since the Great Exhibition of 1851, which, incidentally, the young Morris refused to visit, English taste had been dominated by an eclectic style not dissimilar to the bourgeois taste prevalent in the United States. The furniture of the period was absurdly decorative, with gilt, veneers, and marble used at every opportunity. Moreover, such goods were invariably machine-made and

THE ARTS AND CRAFTS MOVEMENT

LEFT *Wallpaper with Tudor rose and portcullis with initials of Queen Victoria, designed by Pugin for the Houses of Parliament. Pugin's work in the Gothic Revival style ranged from fanciful adaptations to relatively accurate recreations.*

often of very poor quality. The mission of the handicraftsman was a formidable one: to educate and reform public taste and also to reform the means of production and consumption. This socialist aesthetic is neatly summarized in *The Lesser Arts*, in which Morris wrote:

'To give people pleasure in the things they must perforce *use*, that is one great office of decoration; to give people pleasure in the things they must perforce *make*, that is the other use of it.'

Several of the design projects of Morris, Marshall, Faulkner and Co. well illustrated this statement, especially the joint endeavours involving their own domiciles that were undertaken by the firm's principals and assorted friends and relatives.

The firm's first commissions came, predominantly, from the church, and were the result of the High Anglican interest in church ritual and decoration that, in part, had stimulated an interest in Gothic Revivalist architecture. Also, the foundation of the firm had initially prompted fierce opposition from other manufacturers, to the extent that ecclesiastical commissions were one of the few segments of the market to which the company had easy access. Among the earlier commissions were those of the architect G. F. Bodley, who had used stained glass designed by Madox Brown, Burne-Jones and Rossetti for his newly built churches including St Martin's on the Hill, Scarborough, Yorkshire. Morris and Co. had

also decorated other parts of the interior of St Martin's, contributing a painted mural and two painted panels on the pulpit. Other ecclesiastical commissions followed, among them Madox Brown's work for St Oswald's Church, Durham, and one of the few examples of stained glass by Morris himself, for the Church of St Giles in Camberwell, London.

The fortunes of the company were at first precarious. J. W. Mackail, Morris's biographer, mentioned that the firm failed to make any substantial profits during its first years. Its fortunes changed, however, after the International Exhibition of 1862, to which the company contributed specimens of glass, ironwork, embroidery and furniture. Important secular commissions to decorate the Dining Room at the South Kensington Museum (now the Victoria and Albert Museum) and the Tapestry and Armoury Room at St James's Palace followed the exhibition, after which the firm seems to have prospered.

The majority of the company's earlier work was expensive. The South Kensington Museum had complained about the cost of the Green Dining Room and other observers had noted that 'it required a long purse to live up to the higher phases of Morrisean taste.' In addition to this, there were attempts to produce for those of more modest means. Madox Brown produced some items of simply made 'artisan' furniture, objects of straightforward utility with virtually no decoration whatsoever. However, the most famous example of the simpler form of furniture produced by Morris and Co. was the 'Sussex' range of chairs.

LEFT The Red House, one of the first examples of Arts and Crafts architecture, was completed for Morris and his new wife Jane Burden in 1860 by Philip Webb. The style of the house is very simple. The exterior is of the local plain red-brick and is capped by a steeply pitched tile roof reminiscent of domestic Tudor buildings. The general simplicity of the white-washed interior was offset by opulent furniture, painted glass, embroidery and fresco paintings, collaboratively designed by artists and craftsmen associated with the Pre-Raphaelites.

LEFT *The first wallpapers designed by William Morris appeared in the 1860s. The papers emphasize the flatness of the wall and avoid a false illusion of depth. Most, like this 'Willow Boughs' design of 1887, are naturalistic, featuring flowers, birds and beasts, and often juxtapose large- and small-scale motifs.*

RIGHT *Morris's attention to detail included the revival of ancient vegetable dyeing methods in preference to utilizing commercial synthetic dyes. In 1881 Morris & Co. acquired the Merton Abbey Tapestry Works, where Morris installed the dye vats which enabled him to reinstate the technique of indigo discharge printing. The use of indigo to create deep and lasting blues entailed a laborious process of dyeing the fabric, then 'discharging' the pattern with a bleaching agent, and had been superseded in commercial printing by the use of the mineral Prussian Blue dye. Using the original indigo discharge system, Morris created some of his most memorable designs, such as 'Strawberry Thief' and this 'Medway' printed cotton (registered 1885).*

In 1874 Morris began some of his first experiments in dyeing silk and woollen yarns for embroidery. In keeping with the best Arts and Crafts traditions, the dyestuffs came from natural sources such as indigo, cochineal and madder, the latter a dye with unusual chemical properties rendering it difficult to use with consistency and precision. The first of the famous 'Marigold' designs, printed in madder by Thomas Wardle, followed in 1875. Under Wardle's supervision, Morris tried his hand at the craft during the following year, having researched traditional dyeing methods from old French and English technical manuals. It was around this period that Morris also began to experiment with woven textiles and carpets. A French weaver helped set up a Jacquard loom and Morris began research into the tapestry collection at the South Kensington Museum. His designs were often taken from early Renaissance needlework, with Morris expressing a characteristic dislike of the more sophisticated patterns and techniques of the seventeenth and eighteenth centuries.

In 1874 the firm was reorganized under Morris's sole direction. In recent years the company had prospered and began to influence the work of its competitors. Showrooms for its products were opened in 1877 in Oxford Street and the company had also expanded its interests to incorporate commercial weaving, dyeing and printing with its other activities. In 1881 attempts were made to find more spacious premises to accommodate all of the firm's work under one roof, and Morris and Co. moved to Merton Abbey.

Production began at Merton Abbey at the end of 1881 and marked the beginning of one of the firm's most prolific periods. The working conditions described by a number of contemporary observers were nothing short of idyllic. Like the craftsmen and women of the Middle Ages, Morris's workers were, according to one observer, free to interpret and add their own personality to many of the designs. Men were involved in the production of most crafts save carpets, which were handmade by women at the cost to the customer of no less than four guineas per square yard. Morris's

ABOVE *The 'Sussex' range of chairs, also known as the 'Good Citizens' furniture, was based on vernacular designs of country designs dating back to the eighteenth century. Unlike many of the products of Morris & Co., this was a range of cheaper furniture for those of modest means.*

workers apparently went unhurriedly about their respective crafts, striving, unlike similar industries in Victorian society, for standards of excellence and beauty rather than quantity.

By the end of the 1880s, Morris and Co. had become something of a nursery for the Arts and Crafts Movement, with many of its artists and craftsmen going on to work independently or to form guilds or associations inspired by Morris's aesthetic and social ideals. However, the 1880s, the period during which the firm was commercially most successful, also marks an important shift in Morris's opinion on the value of the Arts and Crafts. His interest in the Utopian ideals of the ever-expanding ranks of artists and craftsmen had begun to vacillate. When, for example, T. J. Cobden-Sanderson, a disaffected lawyer eager to work with his hands, entertained the idea of taking up book-binding at Jane Morris's suggestion, the surprised lawyer found Morris scathing about the purpose of some Utopian guilds of printers dedicated to the production of beautiful books.

The firm had originally been established as an antidote to and buttress against the shoddy philistinism of the upper and middle classes, yet, decades after its foundation, little had visibly changed in Victorian society. Industrial society continued to produce shoddy goods and had perversely warmed to, and imitated, Morris's work, often with the aid of machinery. His patrons, moreover, ironically came from that section of society that had some responsibility for perpetuating the social conditions he so hated, for good design made under humane and fulfilling working conditions was – as critics had already noted – nothing if not expensive. Morris eventually realized that the capacity of the arts alone to challenge industrial society was severely limited, and so his attitude to the other ventures in the Arts and Crafts that imitated his example (among them

LEFT *Oak centre table made by Morris & Co. The design is attributed to Philip Webb and George Jack, a pupil of Webb's. It was designed for Clouds in the 1880s or early 1890s.*

LEFT *Morris & Co. whistling kettle made of copper and brass. An example of simplicity of design which anticipates the work of the* Deutscher Werkbund *and the* Bauhaus.

Cobden-Sanderson's 'Dove Press') became, at times, less than enthusiastic. Morris, it appears, still strongly upheld the principles that formed the bedrock of the Arts and Crafts Movement. Beautiful, often simple, handmade objects were invariably preferable to anything that profit-mongering, industrial capitalism could offer, yet Morris continued to nurse the nagging doubt that art on its own was merely a palliative. Action was therefore required in a sphere outside the workshop or studio. In 1883 Morris became involved in radical politics and joined a Marxist organization, the Democratic Federation, and at the end of the following year helped to establish the anti-parliamentary Socialist League with Eleanor Marx and Edward Aveling. Morris, through his experience of Marxist teaching, came to realize that only political action had the ability to challenge industrial capitalism, and that only an open conflict with capitalism could ultimately bring about the social conditions in which art might flourish.

After this political conversion, Morris continued to work in a number of often irreconcilable spheres, some artistic and some political. In the late 1880s Morris founded the Kelmscott Press. More an intense personal interest than a business venture, but somewhat paradoxical in view of his earlier discourse on the production of 'beautiful books', the Press was dedicated to reviving early Renaissance methods of book production and type design. Its work was very labour-intensive. The bindings were often intricately tooled and the paper was handmade in paper moulds that were themselves made by hand. The paper carried watermarks and typefaces to Morris's own design, and he seriously intended to produce his own ink, finding the industrially produced inks available in England rather pallid. The firm of Morris and Co. continued to prosper under the capable direction of George Jack. Morris also remained active in the Socialist League, editing and financing its magazine, *The Commonweal*, until 1890 when, after a schism with an anarchist faction, he established the Hammersmith Socialist Society. He also continued to write poetry and prose. During this period he wrote *News From Nowhere*, the novel that elaborated precisely the revolutionary society to which he had aspired in his art and politics. 'What business have we with art at all', he often asked, 'if we all cannot share it?' This query prompted scores of his followers to embrace socialism with enthusiasm, convinced that design reform was impossible to achieve unless preceded by social, political and economic changes.

RIGHT *Oak cabinet and desk, designed by the architect John Pollard Seddon and decorated by Morris, Marshall, Faulkner & Co. in 1862. The paintings on the main panels represent an allegory of the arts, symbolized by episodes from the honeymoon of René of Anjoy, and were executed by Ford Madox Brown, Dante Gabriel Rossetti and Edward Burne-Jones.*

WILLIAM
DE MORGAN

*William De Morgan
(1839–1917) was
associated with Morris
& Co. from 1863,
designing stained glass
and tiles. In 1872 he
founded his own pottery
and showroom in
Chelsea. His tiles,
dishes, bowls, vases and
bottles often feature
plant, flower and
animal designs.*

Throughout his career, Morris struggled to reconcile his artistic ideals with his political inclinations. His commitment to the creation of products that reflected the highest standards of design and construction seemed constantly at odds with his desire to produce them at a cost that middle-class consumers could afford. His dedication to utilizing the aesthetic and technical skills of craftsmen to their fullest potential, in a Ruskinian atmosphere of 'healthy and ennobling labour', conflicted with the necessity of using machine production wherever possible to eliminate the drudgery of certain tasks and to reduce production costs. It was a dilemma that he never fully resolved while director of Morris & Co., and it continued to plague his followers in the years to come.

Morris died in 1896, having made a major contribution to the practical and intellectual development of the principles of the Arts and Crafts Movement. Although his firm may have been only a qualified success from an economic standpoint, it demonstrated the merits of artistic cooperation and inspired a host of imitators throughout England. In both urban and rural locations, small groups of architects, designers, craftsmen and critics banded together in organizations dedicated to design reform. Many were patterned on medieval guilds, and, as such, established certain aesthetic and technical standards to be maintained by their supporters. The emphasis upon the dignity of labour was in many cases developed through socialist ideals. Some groups assumed educational roles, offering lectures, workshops and classes. Most held regular exhibitions to promote the work of members and to educate public taste.

Ruskin was among the first to institute one such utopian guild community, although his Guild of St George, founded in 1871, was one of the more impractical and unsuccessful of the cluster of communities that developed in the wake of Morris & Co. However, Ruskin's example inspired his ex-pupil Arthur Heygate Mackmurdo to found the more successful Century Guild in 1882, in partnership with Selwyn Image, another of Ruskin's associates. Mackmurdo had trained as an architect but had, in addition, attempted to learn several crafts himself, including brasswork, embroidery

ABOVE *In contrast to other stained-glass work at the time, Morris & Co. adopted a free-flowing style in both lead lines and painting with strong vibrant colours and naturalistic form. Edward Burne-Jones (1833 to 1898) put the firm's ideas into stained-glass designs. 'The Angel Musician' (St Peter and St Paul, Cattistock, Dorset) represents his style.*

and cabinetmaking. The purpose of the Century Guild was to unite the traditionally separate disciplines of architecture, interior design and decoration. Whereas Morris had attempted to level the disciplines of painting and sculpture to the rank of democratic handicrafts, Mackmurdo aimed to raise the status of crafts such as building, fabric design, pottery and metalworking to that of the professionally respectable 'fine' arts.

The work of Mackmurdo and the Century Guild tended to be more eclectic than that of Morris & Co., although it aspired to the same ideal of artists, architects and designers co-operatively undertaking the design of a home and its contents. Unlike many medievalists associated with the Arts and Crafts Movement, Mackmurdo extended his appreciation of historical styles to include Italian Renaissance and even Baroque architecture. His furniture was eccentrically stylized, its essentially conventional forms frequently embellished with a fretwork motif of undulating lines. The sinuous plant motifs of Century Guild furniture and textiles often look forward to the flowing curves of Art Nouveau. Members of the guild included the potter William De Morgan, the designer Heywood Sumner, the sculptor Benjamin Creswick, the textile de-

signer and metalworker H. P. Horne and the metalworker Clement Heaton.

The Century Guild was disbanded in 1888. Mackmurdo continued his work as an architect and, like others in the Arts and Crafts Movement, strayed from work connected with the material fabric of society, its art, architecture and so on, to more theoretical concerns, in this instance monetary theory and sociology.

Selwyn Image, co-founder of the Century Guild, was later active in another fraternity, the Art Workers' Guild, formed in 1884 by pupils of the architect Richard Norman Shaw and still in existence today. This too aimed to raise the status of the applied arts and to breach the division of labour that separated them from institutionalized notions of 'high' art. Like other Arts and Crafts ventures, the Art Workers' Guild sought a handcrafted, well-designed environment in which artists, architects and craftsmen would assume collective responsibility for buildings and their contents, although it lacked the conspicuous sense of social purpose of Morris's movement. Despite its deliberate avoidance of public campaigning, the Art Workers' Guild was to have considerable influence; many of its members played prominent roles in art schools and public administration over the next decade.

BELOW LEFT *Garden façade, Standen, Hollybush, East Grinstead, Sussex, by Philip Webb, 1891 to 1894. This gracious country house reflects Webb's mature style and assumes a 'cottagey' demeanour because of its irregular massing and varied coloration and texture. The prominent tower serves as a transition between a rambling service wing and a symmetrical main block.*

BELOW *Design for two cottages by C.F.A. Voysey, c 1901. Like many Arts and Crafts architects, Voysey conceived his houses as 'total design', aiming to supervise or design every item of their furnishing.*

25

The Guild's reluctance to maintain a public profile led to the foundation in 1888 of the affiliated but more militant Arts and Crafts Exhibition Society. Such well-known Arts and Crafts figures as Crane, Webb, Benson, Cobden-Sanderson, Day, Lethaby and De Morgan were prominent in the Society and its exhibition accommodated the work of other like-minded guilds and crafts' fraternities. The first exhibition included contributions not only from its own members but from the Century Guild, Morris and Co. and C. R. Ashbee's nascent Guild and School of Handicraft. In addition to providing a platform to exhibit works from an ever-expanding body of artisans, the Society's exhibitions also afforded the opportunity for theoretical discussions and practical demonstrations in crafts as diverse as printing, bookbinding, design and tapestry weaving.

In 1890 the firm of Kenton and Co. was founded when several young architects, including Ernest Gimson, Sidney and Edward Barnsley, William Richard Lethaby, Reginald Blomfield and Mervyn Macartney, set out 'to produce the best possible furniture of its time, with the best materials and the best workmanship'. Although this enterprise was forced to close only two years later through lack of capital, Ernest Gimson and the Barnsley brothers went on to pursue the craft ideal successfully with their Gloucestershire furniture business.

Another guild to take up residence in Gloucestershire was Charles Ashbee's Guild and School of Handicraft, founded in 1888. Ashbee lamented that the Arts and Crafts Movement had taken a wrong direction: in 1908 he stated that he wished 'to show that this Arts and Crafts Movement . . . is not what the public has thought it to be, or is seeking to make it: a nursery for luxuries, a hothouse for the production of mere trivialities and useless things for the rich. It is a Movement for the stamping out of such things by sound production on the one hand, and the inevitable regulation of machine production and cheap labour on the other.'

The work produced by the guild was simple in design. Its metalwork, in the form of jewellery, cutlery, plates and vases, was often inspired by medieval sources, with the addition of semiprecious stones and modest decorative devices recalling Art Nouveau. Ashbee, however disliked the association and saw a marked distinction between the guild's high socialist and craft ideals and the self-consciously artistic sensibilities of the Art Nouveau movement. Equally simple was the furniture produced by the guild.

In 1902 the fortunes of the Guild and School of Handicraft changed after it moved from London to Gloucestershire. Ashbee established workshops with some 50 of his craftsmen and their families, and offered local residents classes in his School of Arts and Crafts. Although the rural setting was in keeping with the utopian notion that craftsmen benefited from life in the country, the move may have led to the Guild's downfall, as the distance from urban markets created a difficulty in trading. There was increasing competition from firms using mechanized production techniques, enabling them to undercut the guild's prices. By 1905 it was in financial difficulties, with the year's business returning a loss of almost £1,000, a loss which was virtually doubled the following year, forcing the company into liquidation.

THE GUILD OF HANDICRAFT.

ITS DEED OF TRUST AND RULES FOR THE GUIDANCE OF ITS GUILDSMEN, TOGETHER WITH A BRIEF NOTE ON ITS WORK CARRIED UP TO THE CLOSE OF THE YEAR 1909 AND PREPARED FOR THE USE OF ITS MEMBERS AND FOR THE TRUSTEES, BY C. R. ASHBEE.

LEFT *C. R. Ashbee's Guild of Handicraft was located in Chipping Campden in Gloucestershire. Supporters of these utopian communities believed that the craftsmen benefited from life in the country: there, they could work in a clean, quiet, healthy atmosphere in close proximity to nature while learning traditional methods of hand-craftsmanship from local craftsmen.*

A disciple of William
Morris, Ernest Gimson
(1864–1919) produced
furniture which is
characteristic of the Arts
and Crafts ideal. He
refused to mechanize his
production, believing
that he was working to
produce affordable
furniture for the
ordinary man, although
in practice his furniture
was too inefficiently
produced to be enjoyed
by any but the well-to-
do. The ladderback
chair (right) of about
1895 is highly
traditional in design, as
is the set of oak dining
chairs and dining table
(left), dating from about
1890. In 1902 Gimson
set up the successful
Daneway House
workshops, which
produced his designs for
chamfered and inlaid
furniture, firedogs, iron
sconces and hinges,
often in a cottagey
seventeenth-century
style.

RIGHT *Turquoise matrix,*
gold and enamel brooch,
designed by C. R.
Ashbee for the Guild of
Handicraft, c 1899. In
the shape of a butterfly,
it can also be interpreted
as a somewhat floriform
design.

One of the achievements of the Arts and Crafts Movement was the opening up of opportunities not only for the working man but for hitherto unemployable women. In practice, women workers were largely absent in many of the more famous Craft Guilds, at least as shop-floor producers. However, in 1884 the Home Arts and Industries Association was established. This was a charitable body aiming to protect country crafts and traditions and to encourage rural workers to put their leisure time to good use, teaching metalwork, wood-work, knitting, embroidery and spinning. Its goals were to raise standards of aesthetic taste and to afford ailing parts of the rural economy an alternative source of income through the Victorian ideal of self-help. Founded by one Mrs Jebb, with the support of A. H. Mackmurdo, the Association was run on the whole by upper middle-class women, and women workers were numerous. The Association helped to distribute the work of a number of smaller provincial crafts guilds and adult education associations, among them the Keswick School of Industrial Art. This small design school was established in Cumberland in 1884 and was later to sustain itself as a business venture through the sale of its work.

Another sorority motivated by a patrician concern for the poor was the Royal School of Needlework, in London, established to help women in distressed circumstances to earn a living from needlework. Some idea of the

ABOVE *Liberty & Co. designers included the Scotswoman Jessie M. King, who created this silver and enamel pendant, c 1902.*

RIGHT *Round oak table by Heal & Sons, London. Heals retailed furniture and furnishings to the increasingly affluent middle classes, and like Liberty & Co. combined the Arts and Crafts ideals of simplicity and sobriety with more practical marketing goals.*

nature of the school was given by the American fabric designer Candace Wheeler, who visited it prior to establishing her own counterpart: she is recorded as being shocked to see the strong class divisions between the middle-class organizers and the women workers.

The original craft ideal had been turned on its head as public interest in the beautiful and handmade grew. Resonant Victorian themes of hard work, thrift and a benign and deserving poor upstaged the idealism of the movement by embracing the form of the Arts and Crafts Movement but nothing of its socialist and democratic content. Women of little visible wealth communally producing handicrafts of exceptional quality and beauty could, at first sight, emerge from the literary utopias of the nineteenth century. It is important to remember, however, that the craft ideal emerged in novels such as *News From Nowhere* in the wake of profound change. The Royal School of Needlework, the Langdale linen industry, the Home Arts and Industries Association and many other similar schools supervised by the upper classes functioned in the same oppressive industrial and economic conditions that had led to the emergence of the Arts and Crafts Movement in the first place.

While the craft schools tended to diverge from the Arts and Crafts ideal by the exploitation of manual labour, the business of Liberty & Co., established in 1875 by Arthur Lasenby Liberty, modified the ideal in another direction by exploiting both markets and machinery. Technically, Liberty's factory-made commercial products (some with hand-finishing) cannot be deemed Arts and Crafts, unlike the hand-crafted creations of the various Guilds, yet many of their designs relate to the spirit of the Arts and Crafts Movement. Liberty & Co. managed to produce and distribute couture, fabrics, metalwork and furniture to a wider public than either Morris or his followers. The individual handicraft and creative expression of the artisans disappeared in favour of Liberty's policy of anonymity for his designers, although his employees included some of the most prominent names in Arts and Crafts design of the time.

ABOVE *Silver salt cellar designed by C. R. Ashbee, made by the Guild of Handicraft.*

RIGHT *A Shaker rocking chair, c 1840. The Shaker ('Shaking Quaker') sect, which spread to America from England in 1774 and flourished in the early nineteenth century, believed in the simple life. Their belief in the dignity of labour and the beauty of utility anticipated many of the aesthetic ideals of the Arts and Crafts Movement.*

The Arts and Crafts Movement, initially a British development, gradually spread to the United States. Ruskin's writings had been enthusiastically received by some American painters and critics, but it was not until the Centennial Exposition, held in Philadelphia in 1876, that the application of the Arts and Crafts ethos to American culture was taken seriously.

Just as Britain's Great Exhibition of 1851 had drawn the attention of designers to a loss of direction in the applied arts, the Philadelphia Exhibition demonstrated a failure of the United States to fashion a culture of its own. Much of the industrial arts were dominated by the machine-produced Empire Style, with only a few notable and original examples of American work. These included the work of various Cincinnati potters and the simple, handcrafted Shaker furniture. The Shaker ('Shaking Quaker') sect, which spread to America from England in 1774, had maintained pre-industrial craft traditions which conformed closely to Arts and Crafts ideals. However, it was the British contributions in the Arts and Crafts style to the exhibition which were to have a major impact upon American design thinking.

Jeffrey & Co. (the firm that had printed Morris's first wallpapers), Fairfax Murray, Walter Crane, Richard Norman Shaw and the Royal School of Needlework were amongst these contributors. In addition, the work, and to a lesser extent the ideals, of Morris were becoming increasingly well known in the United States. Morris & Co.'s ironwork and versions of its Sussex chair were commercially distributed and a number of designers confessed to having been influenced by his example.

By 1890 the Arts and Crafts Movement was the most important foreign importation of style to the United States. This encouraged an interest in fine workmanship and a growing awareness of the need for a truly national art. The concepts of a national art, however, differed across the country. On the East Coast Morrisian communities were founded, producing furniture and other decorative items which have a direct resemblance to those of the British movement. In California, Morris's romantic return to the medieval European past was supplanted by a recognition of that state's own past in Spanish-Mexican and Indian culture.

One of the most conspicuous developments in American Arts and Crafts – and one developed again by craftswomen rather than men – occurred in the field of ceramics. Mary Louise McLaughlin, of the influential Cincinnati school of potters, was to evolve what became a characteristically American style of decoration based on a French technique of ceramic underglazing. The same technique was used by Maria Longworth Nichols, founder of the highly successful Rookwood Pottery. As in Britain, the notion that creative work enabled women to turn their hands to a trade both useful and appropriate to their sex was to open up new opportunities for women craftsmen.

With a nationwide demand for, and interest in, Art Pottery, the United States was to make a distinct contribution to this field. Despite the 'good works' of Candace Wheeler, Newcomb College and the Paul Revere Pottery, the missionary zeal associated with creative labour so typical of the British Arts and Crafts tradition is largely absent in most examples of American ceramics.

ROOKWOOD POTTERY

The Rookwood Pottery
of Cincinnati, founded
by Maria Longworth
Nichols in 1880, was
America's foremost
producer of art pottery.
Its wares were often
characterized by
underglazing, a difficult
technique requiring mild
firing to maintain the
warm-coloured glaze.
When the pottery won a
Grand Prix at the 1900
Paris Exhibition, a
craze started for its
elegant wares. Best-
known are perhaps the
vases, decorated with
floral themes
(far left), pictures of
Red Indians, animals
and birds (left).
However, Rookwood's
extensive range
comprised not only
utilitarian vessels but
also landscape plaques
and, from 1902, tiles.
This example
(below left), featuring a
pair of rabbits flanking
a tulip tree, was made
in 1911 and has a high-
gloss glaze rather than
the matt finish usually
employed by
Rookwood.

However, the craft ideal appears in far more robust form in the example of the furniture designer Gustav Stickley. Stickley trained from 1875 in his uncle's chair factory and opened a furniture store in New York in 1883. His earliest work followed the trend for reproduction of European styles, but he felt the abstraction of such traditions from their historical and social context inappropriate. He found himself increasingly drawn towards the quest for an American vernacular style. After visiting Europe in 1898, he started designing aggressively simple furniture, adopting the Shaker ideal of functional beauty. For the average American consumer, he wrote, 'art should not be allowed to remain as a subject of consideration for critics. It should be brought to their homes and become for them a part and parcel of their daily lives.' His aim was 'a simple, democratic art' that should provide ordinary people with 'the material surroundings conducive to plain living and high thinking, to the development of the sense of order, symmetry and proportion.'

Stickley gave attention both to the form of his furniture and the manner in which it was made, setting great store by Morris's demand that the labour of the craftsman should be free and contented. To this end his firm of United Craftsmen, like its British counterparts, attempted to evoke the communal fraternities of the Middle Ages, with a profit-sharing scheme for the craftsmen and regular meetings at the workshops' to secure harmony and unity of effort.' Unlike some Arts and Crafts idealists, Stickley did not bar machinery from the workshops, but it was used only to liberate the workers from unnecessary labour. His 'Craftsman' furniture was highly successful, and frequently publicized in *The Craftsman* magazine which he published from 1901 to 1916. The magazine became the best-known American forum for Arts and Crafts philosophy.

Despite an ignominious end with Stickley's bankruptcy in 1915, United Craftsmen represented a radical departure in the American Arts and Crafts Movement. Stickley had followed not only the outward signs of craftsmanship but also the spirit. The work was pleasing to look at, well and sensibly made by creatively fulfilled craftsmen who were getting something like proper remuneration for their labour. Moreover, Stickley's products owed no stylistic debt to European notions, save that of notions of common-sense craftsmanship pioneered originally by Ruskin and Morris.

His contemporary Elbert Hubbard brought equal enthusiasm to the Arts and Crafts ideal with the Roycroft Press, a publishing business originally inspired by Morris's Kelmscott Press. His early books were poor imitations of Kelmscott products, but Hubbard evidently recognized their deficiencies, and began to employ gifted designers, decorators, printers and binders who contributed to the production of outstanding volumes. In 1901 Roycroft expanded to produce Mission-style furniture similar to that of United Craftsmen, leather and metalwork gifts, simple ceramics and household items. Like United Craftsmen, Roycroft had democratic pretensions. Its catalogue proudly declared that beautiful objects should be available to everyone, although Hubbard's enthusiasm for the Arts and Crafts ideals was condemned by some as naively populist: according to one critic, 'he popularized . . . the Arts and Crafts to the point of vulgarity.'

ABOVE *Print of the Roycroft Shops of Hubbard's crafts community in East Aurora, near Buffalo, New York.*

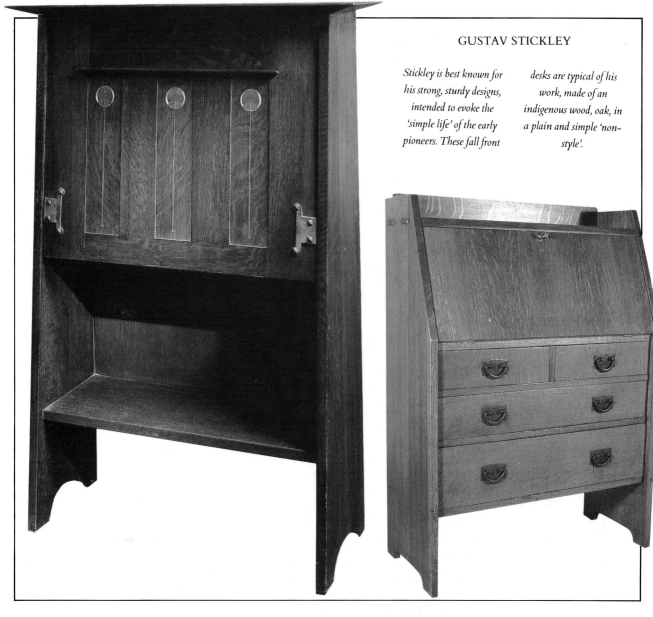

GUSTAV STICKLEY

Stickley is best known for his strong, sturdy designs, intended to evoke the 'simple life' of the early pioneers. These fall front desks are typical of his work, made of an indigenous wood, oak, in a plain and simple 'non-style'.

LEFT *'A Craftsman Dining Room', as featured in* The Craftsman, *USA, Gustav Stickley, c 1904. 'Craftsman' interiors are designed to combine easily mass-produced fittings with a homely and comfortable atmosphere.*

FRANK LLOYD WRIGHT

Frank Lloyd Wright, architect and designer, was a major influence on American Arts and Crafts architecture and the foremost exponent of Prairie School architecture. From 1887 to 1893 he worked in Louis Sullivan's office in Chicago and took over the residential commissions. The Prairie Style houses which followed, such as those for Ward W. Willits (1902 to 1923) and Susan Lawrence Dana (1903), reflected the open, flat geography of Illinois with their strong horizontals and low overhanging roofs. He also designed dark oak furniture, popularizing tall spindle-back chairs and built-in cupboards in his functional, open-plan interiors. His furniture clearly owes a great debt to Rennie Mackintosh. In 1897 he was a founding member of the Chicago Arts and Crafts Society, and by 1900 he had designed more than 50 houses. He went on to become a leading Modernist, and the contrast between the Arts and Crafts buildings and later works such as his Guggenheim Museum (1956 to 1959) well illustrates his diversity.

ABOVE *The Ward Willits House, Highland Park, Illinois, by Frank Lloyd Wright, 1902.*

LEFT *Chair by Frank Lloyd Wright for Ward Willits House, Highland Park, Illinois. Furniture such as this was designed to complement the architectural space.*

RIGHT *Copper 'weed vase', designed by Frank Lloyd Wright, made by James A. Miller, Chicago, c 1894. Dissatisfied with contemporary decorative objects, Wright set about making his own. This flower holder was one of his earlier creations.*

BELOW *This chair in Wright's familiar materials, oak and leather, was designed for the Imperial Hotel in Tokyo, Japan. It is minimalist and geometric in line, based on the hexagon and the octagon, and demonstrates Wright's desire to fit the movable furniture to the spirit of the immovable space in which it is contained.*

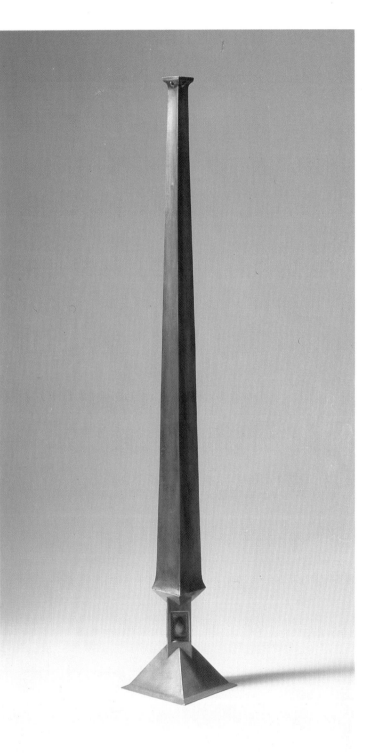

2. ART *nouveau*

LEFT *Corsage ornament by the premier Art Nouveau illustrator, Alphonse Mucha, and goldsmith Georges Fouquet, featuring gold, enamel, emerald and baroque pearl, with the figure painted on mother-of-pearl.*

THE ARTS AND CRAFTS MOVEMENT, AS DIRECTLY CONNECTED WITH MORRIS, WAS ALL BUT DEAD BY THE EARLY TWENTIETH CENTURY. But in the late 1880s a new style was already emerging – Art Nouveau. Where the Arts and Crafts Movement had its roots firmly planted in the past, the essence of Art Nouveau – as its name affirms – was that it was a truly new style.

The essence of Art Nouveau is a line, a sinuous extended curve found in every design of this style. Art Nouveau rejected the order of straight line and right angle in favour of a more natural movement. Whether these lines were used in realistic depictions of natural forms or as abstracted shapes evoking an organic vitality, the emphasis was on decorative pattern and also flatness, a surface on which this concern for the linear, the line of Art Nouveau, could be developed. Solidity, mass, permanence, any connection with weight or stability and stillness ran counter to the Art Nouveau style. The insubstantiality of line was best exploited in light malleable materials, or those that could be fashioned to appear so. It was, in essence, a graphic style of decoration that was transferred on to a variety of solid objects. This curving, flowing line brought with it a feeling of airy lightness, grace and freedom.

The characteristic curving forms of Art Nouveau first appeared in England, yet they were to spread rapidly throughout Europe to a wide range of cities, each with a distinctive interpretation of the style: Paris and Nancy in France, Munich, Berlin and Darmstadt in Germany, Brussels, Barcelona, Glasgow and Vienna all became focal points for the style that was soon universal in Europe, and – with centres in New York and Chicago – equally influential in America. At the time, this range of regional styles resulted in some confusion as to terminology as well as sources. Often it was the theme of modernity that was to provide a name – *Art Nouveau* and *Modern Style* in France, *Modernismo* in Spain and *Moderne Stile* in Italy – or else a simple reference to place as with *Belgische Stil* (Belgium Style) in Germany or *Stile Inglese* in Italy. There was no clear idea

RIGHT *The Art Nouveau style of stained glass is characterized by its swirling asymmetrical naturalism, with clean, sinuous lines often ending in a whiplash, and stylized floral and other organic themes.*

RIGHT *Paris Metro entrance, Victor Hugo, by Hector Guimard, 1900. Guimard's inventively organic cast-iron entrances to the Paris underground were inspired works of fantasy. Their dramatic contrast with the historical dignity of surrounding buildings was highly controversial and infuriated many Parisians.*

LEFT *Pearwood cabinet by Hector Guimard, c 1900. The idiosyncratic inventiveness and sculpted, abstract curvilinear curves seeming to deny the very nature of the material are characteristic of Guimard's high Art Nouveau phase.*

as to a common origin, nor shared characteristics, until the style was in its decline. Only with hindsight has a more coherent view of the period been formed.

The term itself, *Art Nouveau*, derives from the Parisian shop of the same name run by a German emigré, Samuel Bing. Bing had been trading for ten years in Japanese art when, in 1895, he re-opened his premises as *La Maison de l'Art Nouveau* and started to show the work of contemporary designers as well as painters and sculptors. This mixture of gallery, shop and showroom became the Parisian base for the new style, encouraging Bing to commission works for the shop and to promote his artists and craftsmen abroad. Another Italian term for the style, *Stile Liberty*, was a tribute to Liberty & Co., the London department store whose designers took up the new style in much the same way as they had popularized Arts and Crafts themes.

This mixture of commerce and art, so suitable for the Art Nouveau interest in household artefacts, was not restricted to a few enlightened retailers, but is best seen in the way the style spread through the great international trade fairs of the era. Public interest was also reflected in the great number of new periodicals devoted to Art Nouveau trends. The German version of the style, *Jugendstil*, even derived its name from the influential Munich-based journal *Jugend* (youth), while also sometimes being called *Studiostil* after the widely read English, and later American, periodical *The Studio*. Equivalent publications were *Pan* from Berlin and *Ver Sacrum* from Vienna. The main coverage of the new style appeared less in specific articles than in the actual design of the publications themselves, with title-pages, typefaces and illustrations by Art Nouveau graphic artists. Through exhibitions, shops, galleries and magazines the Art Nouveau style spread rapidly throughout Europe and America, both feeding off and stimulating the public's interest.

'New art' this may have been, yet its origins can be found in Victorian England. The work of a number of designers anticipates the appearance and theoretical basis of the style. The rejection of mass-production in favour of a return to craftsmanship is common with the Arts and Crafts Movement. As early as 1862 the potency of eccentric curves was recognized by the Victorian ornamental designer Christopher Dresser, who wrote: 'A section of the outline of an ellipse is a more beautiful curve than that of the arc since its origin is less apparent, being traced from two centres.

The fascination with natural forms that informs Art Nouveau design also harks back to the Arts and Crafts Movement, although these forms were used for different ends. Where Morris and his co-designers had adopted curving natural shapes to simplify and integrate them into their overall designs, Art Nouveau stylized and exaggerated that same source. The quasi-naif naturalism of Morris's dumpy speckled thrushes or symmetrically ordered flowers gives way to an increasing elongation and elegance. Jean-Auguste Dampt, of the Nancy School, defined the role of natural forms in Art Nouveau inspiration when he wrote, 'art is the essence of Nature refined, purified and synthesized, through the medium of an artist's temperament, which should not copy it, but transform and stylize it.'

By common consensus, the first true example of Art Nouveau design is to be found in the work of Arthur Mackmurdo. Influenced by the flowing, natural forms of Morris, Mackmurdo developed these shapes into elongated, increasingly elegant patterns and was the first to produce the characteristic vocabulary of Art Nouveau. The breakthrough is seen to be Mackmurdo's illustration for the title page of his book, *Wren's City Churches*. As early as 1883 Mackmurdo had created the sinuous, flame-like shapes that were to be the hallmark of Art Nouveau for the next 20 years.

The ideals of Morris, promoting the notion of artist as craftsman, who would revitalize society as a whole, were equally important to the development of Art Nouveau. As a style Art Nouveau therefore owed its origin to the earlier English Crafts.

ABOVE *Title page for Mackmurdo's* Wren's City Churches, *1883. The flame-like tendrils of Mackmurdo's illustration had an almost violent quality that was subsequently modified by many of his followers.*

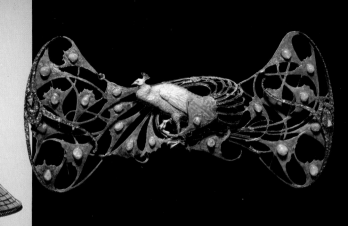

NATURAL FORMS

*Nature was the ultimate
source book of the Art
Nouveau artist. Flowers,
stems and leaves were
chosen for their curving
silhouettes: lilies, irises
and orchids were
favoured, although any
and every form, offered
potential for
development, as seen in
this etagère (right) by
Emile Gallé with
intricate dragonfly
support, standing lamp
(left) by Louis Comfort
Tiffany with dragonfly
shade, and peacock
corsage (above) ornament
by René Lalique.*

Not all stylistic features can be traced so easily to one source, nor despite the apparent modernity of the movement, are they devoid of historical links. Despite the anti-revivalist, novel qualities of Art Nouveau, some of the strands of its complicated and extensive root structure were grounded in the revival of past styles. The Gothic Revival served in some ways as an inspiration, for the fervent examination of medieval art of the mid-nineteenth century had emphasized the value of curving, organically inspired shapes seen in the architecture, sculpture and stained glass of the Middle Ages, contrasting to the rectilinear severity of Classicism. Both Ruskin and Morris had turned to the medieval artists' study of nature as their inspiration and their interest was reflected in that of their contemporaries, the Pre-Raphaelite painters.

Dante Gabriel Rosetti and Edward Burne-Jones, leading Pre-Raphaelites, both designed and painted furniture for Morris as well as including specific details of dress and armour in their paintings. As this kind of historical appreciation of Gothic grew, so too did the awareness that this term encompassed a number of different styles, from the chaste, plain lines of its early period to the flamboyant fantasy of later medieval art. It was this form of the style that was to inspire the Art Nouveau. Stained glass, too, immediately reminiscent of the Middle Ages and revived by the Arts and Crafts workers, was also to play an important part in Art Nouveau design. The late Gothic style was plundered not to afford pedantic historical details, but as a sourcebook for new ideas.

Viollet-le-Duc differed from Ruskin in his acceptance of new industrially-produced materials in art, particularly the use of iron in architecture. Another Frenchman offers a striking parallel to both Ruskin and Morris; Léon de Laborde, the organizer of the French entry in the 1851 Great Exhibition. Laborde's report on the Exhibition criticized the gap that had been created between the arts and mechanically-produced artefacts. To correct this, he advised artists to concern themselves in future less with reviving the trappings of past styles and more with the design of everyday objects. These very

DE LA COUR DU CHATEAU DE CHARLEVAL

ABOVE *Illustration from Viollet-le-Duc's* Entretiens sur l'Architecture *(1863–72).*

BOTTOM RIGHT *A detail from the Amalienburg revealing the curling leaf forms of Rococo. Instead of reviving the style, designers re-examined this decorative use of naturally inspired forms for their own purposes.*

BELOW *The flamboyant late Gothic style, seen here in window tracery on the west front of York Minster, served as an inspiration to Art Nouveau designers.*

Morris-like ideas were echoed by Viollet-le-Duc in his teaching at the Parisian Ecole-des Beaux-Arts, where he recommended far closer collaboration between all the arts, focusing on architecture, to produce a stylistically harmonious whole. With these two men, French Art Nouveau could look to its own theorists and writers for inspiration.

If flamboyant late Gothic provided an example of the creative use of the past by the Art Nouveau, then so too did the inspired re-examination of the eighteenth-century Rococo style in France. This style had become one of the many open to revivalists of the next century, but rather than resurrect it completely, Art Nouveau observed its forms and characteristics with an independent eye. Rococo had been more broadly associated with use of a capriciously cavorting light and delicate line as an ornament in all the decorative arts. This was very close to the line of Art Nouveau, and the connection became clear when, in France, the designers of the regional Nancy school began to incorporate references to Rococo in their work. The common source of natural forms of plant and wave in both Art Nouveau and Rococo made the blend harmonious. The Rococo preference for light, high-keyed colour in interiors was also pursued by Art Nouveau, in reaction to the heaviness and solemnity of sombre Victorian interiors. While it was strongest in France. Munich had also been an important outpost of Rococo in the eighteenth century, and it is no coincidence to find that the lightest, wittiest and most fanciful forms of Jugendstil were later to be found in that city in the work of Hermann Obrist (1863–1927) or August Endell (1871–1925).

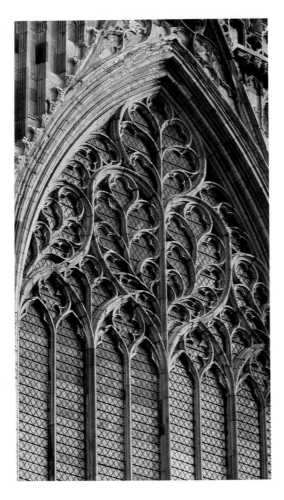

Although Art Nouveau was far removed from the rather naïve and concentrated revivalism that had preceded it, its designers drew from previous centuries for inspiration, and in particular were attracted by the flowing curvilinear designs of early Celtic and Nordic art. Celtic jewellery, stonework and the splendidly illuminated early medieval gospel Books of *Durrow*, *Lindisfarne* and *Kells* revealed in their elaborately curving and twisting decoration precisely the combination of stylization and natural inspiration that typified Art Nouveau itself. The Art Nouveau love of an undulating line had a natural affinity with the Celtic predilection for interlaced and spiral patterns and for stylized, elongated plant and animal motifs. In particular, the work of such artists as Archibald Knox, Charles Rennie Mackintosh and other members of the Glasgow School clearly recalls the typically Celtic contrast of lavish and exuberant ornament confined within strict limits and set against more open areas. Interest in Celtic art is evident in Liberty's 'Cymric' silverware launched in 1899 and in their range of tableware and jewellery which makes copious use of the Celtic interlace patterns.

An interest in early Nordic art in the Scandinavian countries emphasized their revived artistic vitality, and the intricate curves and spirals of this tradition found their way into the local form of Art Nouveau, as in the designs of the Norwegian Henrick Bull. Viking art made vigorous use of a range of sinuous, elongated dragon-like beasts whose ribbon-like bodies weave complex yet orderly patterns. Scandinavian Art Nouveau was occasionally termed the Dragon Style in deference to its Viking source. Morris himself had toyed with this style after several trips to Iceland, as well as translating a number of Viking sagas.

With its capricious use of the past and peculiar mixture of styles, Art Nouveau could not be anything other than a uniquely 'novel' style. Its eclecticism extended to its strong roots in oriental art, and in particular that of Japan. Japan was a relatively new discovery for the West, having been opened up to Western trade in 1853. Some of the leading figures of Art Nouveau began their involvement in the decorative arts as champions of the new Japanese style. When Liberty & Co. opened in 1875 it was to sell Japanese and oriental goods, while Samuel Bing of the Maison de l'Art Nouveau had for years been one of the leading oriental dealers in Paris, with an extensive personal collection of oriental art. Artists such as Gallé, Lalique and Tiffany owed an overt debt to *japonisme*.

The formal links between Japanese prints and Art Nouveau are strong: the emphasis on decorative line, creating flat, patterned work, and the delicate balance between decoration and background were immediately found to be sympathetic. The curving, flowing Japanese line was drawn from observation of nature, filtered through a developed design sense to create more abstracted forms and patterns with the precise degree of artificiality that the Art Nouveau artists found so attractive.

LEFT *Many English Arts and Crafts designers were inspired by the motifs of the Middle Ages. The Celtic entrelac was often used by Archibald Knox, as seen in this silver purse frame set with turquoise matrix.*

OPPOSITE LEFT *Silver biscuit (cookie) box by Archibald Knox using Celtic and Nordic interlacing patterns.*

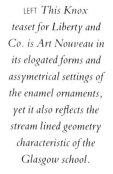

LEFT *This Knox teaset for Liberty and Co. is Art Nouveau in its elogated forms and assymetrical settings of the enamel ornaments, yet it also reflects the stream lined geometry characteristic of the Glasgow school.*

BELOW *The influence of the Orient was equally strong in Art Nouveau Design, resulting in works such as Lalique's elaborate cock's head diadem. The costly materials (gold, enamel and amethyst) and exquisite and intricate craftsmanship are typical of many Art Nouveau luxury items*

CHARLES RENNIE
MACKINTOSH

England was unresponsive to the Art Nouveau style in furniture, but Britain as a whole was represented by Scottish designers, and in particular the Glasgow school. In furniture, as in architecture, it was Mackintosh's work that dominated. Mackintosh's furniture is intended to be seen as part of a whole interior design with secondary work often designed by other artists and designers. As such it has many similarities with his architecture.

In England, Mackintosh's designs were regarded with suspicion for being too stylized, or 'aesthetic', and certainly his furniture is created more for an aesthetic effect than for either comfort or to display the natural quality of the materials. As in his architecture, he concentrated upon extremely elegant, exaggerated verticals, particularly in the backs of his chairs which could be exceptionally tall and slender. These were cut into ovals, grids or ladderbacks that descended down to the floor. Curves might occur, but with Mackintosh they were

primarily used to stress the rigidity of verticals.

Mackintosh felt uncomfortable with the natural grain of the wood and attempted to minimalize it by deep, dark staining and eventually by lacquering or ebonizing it into matt black. He explored a converse neutrality by painting other pieces white to act as a suitable background for lilac and silver harmonies. On lighter furniture, Mackintosh stencilled stylized designs.

CENTRE *Doors for the Willow tea rooms, Glasgow.*

ABOVE *Table and
chair with stencilled
canvas back, c 1901.*

LEFT *Writing
cabinet made for
Mackontosh's study to
his own design; it is
shown open to reveal
pigeonholes and shelves
over the writing surface,
with an open folio stand
below. The stark
angular design, relieved
by the sparkle of small
pieces of glass and
mother-of-pearl, is
typical of Mackintosh's
work, as is the
distinctive glass and
metal flower panel at
the centre of the cabinet.*

Perhaps nowhere are the diversities of Art Nouveau better displayed than in its furniture. Art Nouveau furniture bears all the variety of the regional styles of the movement. True to the spirit of the movement, few craftsmen specialized exclusively in furniture; and most had been trained in other arts or crafts. Most Art Nouveau furniture makers had been, or remained, architects, concerned to extend their control into the interiors of their buildings. The same tensions between ornament and structure, form and function were evident in furniture making as they were in architecture.

In Paris, Samuel Bing's 'Galerie de l'Art Nouveau' was the principal showcase for Art Nouveau furniture, as for other crafts. Reflecting the nationalism fashionable in France at the time, Bing encouraged the craftsmen who worked for him to study the great French tradition of 'grace, elegance, purity and sound logic', and principally the refined poise of eighteenth-century work. The Parisian Art Nouveau designers tended to avoid the more overtly floral detailing of Nancy and concentrated instead on a purity of light and a flowing line. Bing showed a great range of work, but he favoured a nucleus of three furniture makers: Eugène Gaillard, Georges de Feure and Edward Colonna.

Gaillard represents the functional side of Art Nouveau furniture; he studied the problem of function in design and produced designs of an increasingly light, almost classic, simplicity. His chairs were concerned with comfort, had moulded backs, sometimes padding at the shoulder, and leather or fabric-covered coil-sprung, upholstered seats. Georges de Feure, a painter and poet, brought more colour and decoration to his furniture, with gilding and coloured lacqueur, as well as the kind of carved detail rare in Gaillard's work. The third, Edward Eugène Colonna, had emigrated from Cologne to America where he worked under Tiffany, before returning to Europe to continue his career in Paris. Colonna's furniture, like de Feure's was part of a larger output including porcelain and fabrics, and had a delicate, attenuated elegance also close to de Feure's style. When Bing was honoured with his own pavilion devoted to Art Nouveau at the 1900 Paris

ABOVE *Occasional table by Hector Guimard, revealing the same rather taut, skeletal structure as his ironwork, particularly that of the Paris Metro designs.*

World's Fair, these three designers were given the task of decorating and furnishing it.

But much of the vitality of Art Nouveau derived from various provincial centres. In France, the decorative arts were not confined to Paris, but also flourished in the city of Nancy in Lorraine, the home of the glass-making industry. The leader of the Art Nouveau revival of Nancy's main industry was Emile Gallé (1846–1904), heir to a small ceramic and glassware business. Gallé travelled to England in the 1870s and had been caught up in the growing enthusiasm for the decorative arts. He also studied the oriental art collection of the Victoria and Albert Museum in London and, with his new found knowledge of Chinese and Japanese techniques, he returned to Nancy to revitalize his father's workshop. Gallé possessed a specialist's knowledge of botany and entomology, which combined with the decorative, abstract tendency of the Japanese to form the Art Nouveau blend. A third ingredient, Rococo, was already evident in Nancy, which had many fine houses and decorations in that style.

In 1884, after some years of working in glass and ceramics, Gallé started designing and producing furniture. At first his designs were somewhat ponderous but invariably enlivened with vivid natural details. Success came at the 1889 Paris International Exhibition, where Gallé was acknowledged as an innovator, creating a new style in reaction to the unimaginative revivalism of contemporary French furniture. Gallé's work became increasingly lighter and more ornate. Natural forms were not restricted to detail; whole arms, legs and backs were carved in plant or insect forms, curving and twisting to animate the whole and seeming to defy the nature of the wood itself. Gallé preferred soft woods, of which he had a very thorough knowledge, to facilitate the creation of his effects, which included his remarkable revival of the art of marquetry. Most of the surfaces of Gallé's furniture became fields for the most intricate inlays featuring plants, insects or landscapes in what could become an overloading of effects. So fine was the craftsmanship, though, that Gallé's own willowy signature could be reproduced on his pieces.

Gallé was the inspiration behind a couple of craftsmen, termed the Nancy School, who became a loosely formal group in 1901 with the foundation of the Alliance Provinciale des Industries d'Art (1859–1926). Second to Gallé was Louis Majorelle who trained as a painter but then concentrated on running his family's furniture business in Nancy. Majorelle began designing in an eighteenth-century style until persuaded by Gallé to inject a more vital naturalism into his work. His pieces are, nevertheless, rather more solid than Gallé's, partly because he favoured the use of harder, more exotic woods. The more sculptural elements in Majorelle's pieces come in the ornamentation, which, still partly inspired by the Baroque and Rococo, he added in gilt, copper or bronze. Majorelle equalled Gallé in the quality of his marquetry, but generally his style differs in its smoother lines. Majorelle was consequently able to make a successful transition to the simpler style of the 1920s.

BELOW *Art Nouveau walnut armchair attributed to Georges de Feure. A very restrained example of Georges de Feure's work. The chair, although based on a fluid, curvilinear form, has a fairly conventional structure and is more overtly Art Nouveau in the textile design.*

Other Nancy furniture designers of note were Jacques Gruber, Eugène Vallin and Emile André, all of whom became members of the 'Ecole de Nancy, Alliance Provinciale des Industries d'Art' founded by Gallé in 1901. Gruber, during the late 1890s, showed an interest both in glass and in furniture, working for the Daum brothers and designing furniture for Majorelle. He ran his own cabinetmaking business for ten years between 1900 and 1910, creating pieces which, at their best, exploited to the full the abstract sculptural possibilities of French Art Nouveau, but which, at their worst, mixed heavy sculptural themes with naturalistic motifs with an overpowering effect. Gruber's interest in glass can be seen in his use of cameo glass panels in his furniture. After 1910 he devoted all his energies to work in another favoured medium, stained glass.

Eugène Vallin worked for Gallé and produced pieces of a far greater weight than those of his master. His work eschews intricate natural detail and instead concentrates on broad, swaying, linear rhythms, his furniture appearing to grow from the ground in flowing, unbroken lines. Abandoning furniture design, Vallin eventually turned to architecture and satisfied his sculptural interests in work in poured concrete. Emile André, architect and furniture designer, was a founder member of the Ecole de Nancy. Victor Prouvé, friend and associate of Gallé and, after Gallé's death, artistic director of his factory, specialized in marquetry work and created designs for marquetry panels for Gallé and for Majorelle as well as designing his own pieces.

RIGHT *Gallé's* Aube et Crepuscule *('Dawn and Dusk'), the bed he designed while dying of leukemia, was his last great work, eradicating much of the over-intricacy of his earlier pieces, as well as being a tour de force of marquetry. The end of the bed and the headboard are dominated by huge moths with outspread wings portrayed in a rich mix of veneers: most exotic of all are bands of mother-of-pearl mosaic laid into their wings to recreate their silvery sheen. The jaws of the giant moth at the end of the bed hold a large oval drop of glass, itself etched with moths. Beneath the wings of the moth on the bedhead is a night landscape depicted in an array of fruitwood marquetry with gold-dust seemingly scattered over it by the moth. The bed, designed in 1904, was intended to celebrate the wedding of a close friend and patron, Henry Hirsch.*

LEFT *Mantelpiece by Eugène Vallin.*

ABOVE *French pearwood chair by Hector Guimard, c 1900. This chair shows many hallmarks of the Nancy school of design, with its curvaceous lines and elegance.*

RIGHT *Office suite, consisting of a desk, matching chair and sideboard, by Eugène Vallin, in the exaggerated Art Nouveau style known in France as Style Liberty.*

Architecture provides a backdrop against which all the varied creations of Art Nouveau can be set. The interdependence between the fine and decorative arts in Art Nouveau is best seen via the work of the major architects of the time, who required fittings in keeping with their domestic architecture while their fellow craftsmen needed the appropriate setting to display their work. From among the fine arts it is architecture that has the strongest technical, craft base, and when the conventional crafts were on the decline in the face of industrialization, architects were at the forefront of their revival. William Morris, his colleague Philip Webb, and Arthur Mackmurdo were all trained architects. Many of the leaders of Art Nouveau were also architects: Horta, Guimard, Van de Velde, Behrens, Mackintosh, Gaudi, Gaillard and Grasset.

RIGHT *Antoní Gaudi, Barcelona, Casa Mila, 1905–7.*

LEFT *Paris Metro, Bois de Boulogne, by Hector Guimard, 1900.*

RIGHT *Antoní Gaudi, Barcelona, detail of window, Casa Mila, 1905–7.*

The versatility of use and range of metals available meant that almost every Art Nouveau designer turned his hand to metalwork at some stage. They employed the complete range of metals, at times mixing them with other materials such as enamel, ivory, wood or tortoiseshell to create the desired effect. Two extremes typifying the spirit of the movement are the architectural use of wrought iron, and the use of precious metals in intricate and original jewellery.

Wrought iron was a significant part of Art Nouveau architecture, both structurally and decoratively, serving as a link between the building itself and the style of its contents. From exterior balconies, gates and window mullions it continues to the interior in columns, beams, banisters, door handles and even to furniture embellishments. The Belgian architect Victor Horta pioneered the Art Nouveau style with dramatic use of ironwork in his Hotel Tassel, designed in 1892, exposing the load-bearing iron columns in the hall and stairwell, and giving them a treatment entirely Art Nouveau in character by shaping them to resemble the stems of some fantastic vegetation, with numerous twisting metal fronds at the capital level. Having mastered the 'whiplash' line, Horta applied it extensively in the elaborate iron staircases and balconies of buildings such as his Hotel Solvay (1894) and the Maison and Atelier Horta (1898 to 1900).

Unlike Horta, Hector Guimard worked in cast as well as wrought iron, and it was the former that provided the material for his famous shelters and archways for the entrances to the underground stations of the Paris Metro, so startingly Art Nouveau in their conception that they provoked considerable controversy. The treatment of the ironwork was typically curvilinear, with barely a straight line: lamps sprouted from metal branches, and the word 'Metropolitain' itself was composed into harmonious Art Nouveau shapes. Some of these ironwork shapes, although organic in feel, had an angular tension strangely reminiscent of bones and lacked the fluid grace of much of Guimard's interior designs, and of French Art Nouveau as a whole. Their originality even resulted in a local variation of Nouveau design, the '*style Metro*'.

ABOVE *Victor Horta built the Maison et Atelier Horta, a house and studio adjacent to each other, in Brussels, 1898–1900. His adventurous use of ironwork with typical Art Nouveau curves is demonstrated in the elaborate balconies of his house.*

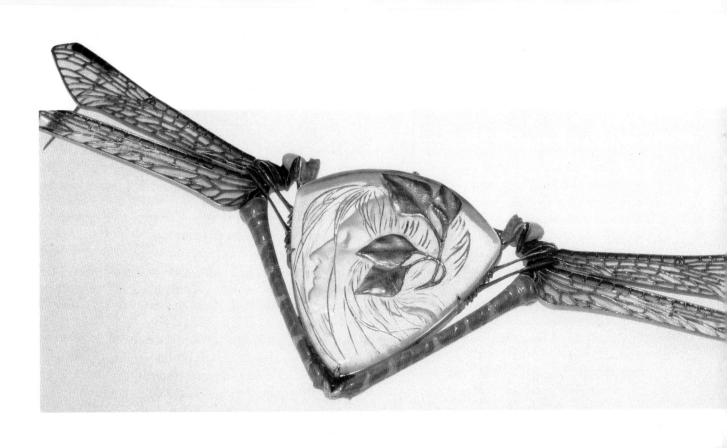

In Spain, Antoni Gaudi, arguably the most original and accomplished of Art Nouveau architects, made extravagant use of decorative ironwork. In his first work, the Casa Vicens (1878–1880), striking wrought-iron gates and railings are modelled on a pattern of palm fronds. By 1905, when he began two apartment blocks, the Casa Batlió and the Casa Milá, he was producing bizarrely undulating masonry with intricately twisted wrought-iron balconies forming an integral part of the design.

At the opposite extreme from architectural use of ironwork is the delicate use of precious metals by Art Nouveau jewellers. Typically these were mingled with semiprecious and nonprecious gems and metals as well as glass, horn, tortoiseshell and enamelling. Without doubt, the Frenchman René Lalique was the master goldsmith of the Art Nouveau era. His jewellery covers the entire repertoire of Art Nouveau themes and inspiration, with brightly plumaged peacocks, glistening-shelled beetles, tensely coiled enamel serpents, realistically rendered flowers and trees, exotic, graceful women and tightly embracing couples.

TOP *Brooch/cloak clasp in gold, glass and* plique-à-jour *enamel, by Lalique, c 1904–5.*

ABOVE *Dog collar, in gold, enamel, glass and pearls, by Lalique, c 1900.*

The great innovators of Art Nouveau glass were French and American. The first was Joseph Brocard who studied Islamic art and restored Arab artefacts in order to learn more about the way they had been made. He was particularly interested in the colour effects that the Islamic craftsmen brought to their glassware through their use of coloured enamel finishes. Brocard's line of thought was followed and developed to its utmost by a series of brilliant technical innovations by Emile Gallé.

Gallé began by exploring the possibilities of colour, at first translucent, as in the 'clair de lune' glass with its delicate sapphire tinge and then, in 1889, opaque colour, which made a greater range possible. Continually experimenting with new techniques to achieve a range of new effects, he developed relief effects by moulding the glass, adding further coatings, by using acid to strip down layers, or by embedding elements such as gold dust or enamel within the glass itself. Experimentation with the production process led to the creation of deliberate crazing in quartz, producing delicate, coloured veins as a feature rather than a flaw, and to the incorporation of bubbles in the glass to imitate raindrops or the dew on an orchid's petals. Gallé revived ancient techniques such as the ancient Roman use of cased glass, in which layers of different colours are fused together and part of the top layer cut away to create a cameo effect. He invented the technique of *marquetrie-sur-verre*, the blending of semi-molten layers of glass on a semi-molten body. The sculptural quality of this inspired Gallé to experiment with a more three-dimensional approach to glassware, and in his later work he created a new range of forms by experimenting with the actual shape of the glassware itself, rather than just the surface.

Gallé's designs were frequently informed by his great interest in and knowledge of botany and natural history – the motto over his workshop door was 'My roots are deep in the woods.' The flowers and plants on his vases are highly naturalistic and are allowed to dictate the form of the glassware rather than being adapted to fit; he also employed dragonflies, frogs, even micro-organisms in his designs. Another source of inspiration was poetry, and his *verreries parlantes* ('talking glassware') were inscribed with lines from writers such as Baudelaire and Hugo, coupled with appropriate images.

Gallé led a renaissance of the glass industry in Nancy. Perhaps the greatest of his imitators were the brothers Auguste and Antonin Daum. The Daum brothers were able to employ some of the talented designers working at Nancy, such as the versatile Jacques Gruber. They too were concerned with opacity, colour and relief, using acid to eat away layers of glass to reveal hidden colour beneath, or powdered enamel fused on to the surface to create a glowing, opaque finish. They were also involved with the revival of *pâte-de-verre*, an opaque, alabaster-like form of glassware produced by using ground-down glass. Other glassware designers of the period included Eugène Rousseau, who used reliefs, inscriptions, tracery crazing in glass, gold leaf and flecks. His most original work was using glass to imitate gemstones apparently set into his glass vessels.

BELOW *The Daum brothers were glassmakers whose work is clearly influenced by Gallé and who achieved a consistenly high standard, decorating the surface of their glassware with a charm and lightness of intention that is sometimes missing in Gallé's serious statements.*

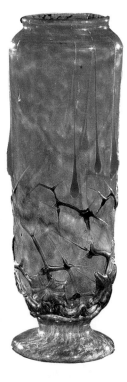

INTRODUCTION TO THE DECORATIVE ARTS

Gallé's mastery of glassmaking techniques enabled him to produce a staggering range of effects. His cameo glasswork, engraving two or more layers of glass fused together, was inspired by a study of ancient Roman glassware: delicate and subtle effects could be achieved, as in this vase (below right) featuring dragonflies above a lily pond. He also experimented with enamelling on glass (below far left). The technique of marquetrie sur verre was his own invention, inspired by his work with marquetry on wood; shaped pieces of hot glass are pressed into the body of a glass object of contrasting colour, the resulting surface being flat, and the inlaid pieces often further decorated with engraving. The marquetrie sur verre vase (above right) is engraved with irises, a favourite flower. Gallé's verreries parlantes ('talking glassware) are works featuring quotations from writers he admired. The brush-holder (above left) was one of his first essays in this form.

LOUIS COMFORT
TIFFANY

Louis Comfort Tiffany was the American designer who rivalled Gallé as a craftsman in glass. Tiffany came from a family of goldsmiths and jewellers and produced work in both these media, but after a study trip to Paris he began contrating upon glassware. The Tiffany Glass & Decoration Company, founded in 1879, rapidly became a very successful enterprise, its most prestigious commission being the decoration of rooms in the White House.

With the opening of a new glassworks at Corona, Tiffany began producing what he called Favrile, or handmade glass goods. These exploited the use of chemical soaks or vapours to create different surface textures from matt to a burnished glow, and a variety of rich colours.

Tiffany's glass rarely has the modelled plasticity of Gallé or Daum; its decoration, more abstract in its depiction of natural forms, rarely rises out in relief but appears to be more of an applied surface pattern. The silhouette of a Tiffany vase thus remains simple and elegant,

although to complement the simplified decoration the vase shapes themselves are more adventurous, often stretched up on impossibly slender, plant-like stems or with twisting serpentine necks inspired by the works of the ancient Persian craftsmen. Unlike the Nancy School, Tiffany's glass never attempts to imitate gems, water, petals or any other natural objects. Like Gallé, Tiffany's success encouraged a crop of imitators, chief among whom were the Quezal Art Glass & Decorating Company of Brooklyn, and Handel & Company of Connecticut.

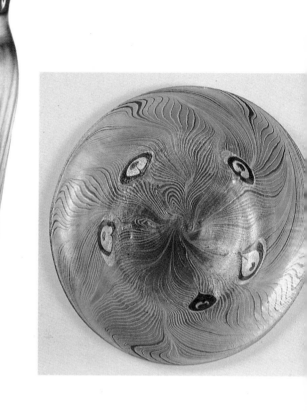

58

RIGHT *Organic forms, a constant motif in Art Nouveau, were employed by Tiffany in a range of elegant flower form vases with slender stems. His 'Jack-in-the-Pulpit' vases proved the ideal shape with which to display his iridescent glass, whose silky tactile quality, inspired by the sheen of ancient Roman glass, was never rivalled by any of his imitators.*

BELOW LEFT *Mosaic and bronze lotus table lamp with Favrile glass shade by Tiffany Studios.*

LEFT *Glass plate by Tiffany using the peacock feather motif, a favourite Art Nouveau device.*

OPPOSITE FAR LEFT *'Goose-necked' vase by Tiffany, inspired by a Persian perfume flask.*

The development of the incandescent electric lamp by Thomas Edison in the 1880s posed a new challenge for designers, although it is typical of a tendency in Art Nouveau that the modernity and startlingly technological aspect of the electric light were ignored by many designers in favour of a more romantic treatment, with the use of organic forms and coloured glass shades. Tiffany, Gallé and Daum all produced lamps as part of their glassware range. Indeed, Tiffany's name was to become synonymous with a style of lamp which used coloured glass set into leaded panels exactly like a conventional stained-glass window. The glass shades might be designed as flowers in a conventional shape. In the Wisteria Lamp, each fragment of glass is a leaf while the moulded metal stem and base formed the trunk and roots.

In designs by Majorelle, Guimard, Gallé or Valin, sinuous metal plants or saplings are created which flower into electric bulbs. The electric light is used in the same manner as the precious stone in a piece of Art Nouveau jewellery: the whole setting, whether it is a vine, thistle, a sprig of mistletoe or a lily, constitutes the bulk of the work, while the electric globes are scattered around the metalwork as highlights. While the majority of Art Nouveau lamps feature glowing flowers, the bronze or gilt statuettes of nymph-like figures produced by many craftsmen could also be

BELOW *Stained-glass window by Jacques Gruber for a medical school in Nancy, France. Gruber was Professor of Decorative Arts in the city, at the Ecole des Beaux-Arts. He was part of the renaissance of the glass industry in Nancy, headed by Gallé and the Daum brothers, and showed the same concern for opacity, colour and relief.*

BELOW *Gallé lamp with overlay of butterfly and sycamores. The use of the mushroom shape was quickly adopted as the most analogous form in nature.*

adapted to carrying an electric light, providing rather a coy interplay between ornamentation and function. They have an escapist charm, but to the eyes of a future generation of designers they would show only a retreat into impractical fantasy, at odds with the nature of the artefact itself. From the range of Art Nouveau craftsmen and designers only Henry van de Velde, commissioned by Bing, produced an electric lamp that took as its starting point the practical and scientific nature of the medium.

A more traditional part of glass design was that of stained glass, a medium that was perfectly suited to the flatness, linearity and love of light and colour that were common to all the contemporary decorative arts. Also a designer often wanted to control the light cast on his interior by making it harmonize with the flowing plant forms of the furniture, wallpaper and table ornaments.

Stained glass was widely manufactured and used to some degree in very wealthy homes of the period, yet most Art Nouveau stained glass was not representative of a high level of craftsmanship, but consisted of regularly shaped, painted or enamelled panes, easy to produce and assemble. Only in the best quality designs was the traditional method of production retained, in which each motif was carefully outlined in lead, using panels of differing shapes and sizes. In Nancy, Jacques Gruber produced his stained glass of exquisitely-observed plants, flowers and birds in this way, as did Guimard in Paris. Guimard's stained glass, like his ironwork, was designed as part of an architectural whole, and one sees in his windows the same abstract arches, bows and ripples as can be seen in the ironwork of his gates.

LEFT *Stained glass was not only used for windows and door panels, in which form it decorated everything from small suburban houses to stately mansions, but was also made into ornamental pieces and insets for furniture, as in this longcase clock by Jacques Gruber.*

3. ART *deco*

THE TERM ART DECO DESCRIBES, IN A SOMEWHAT SIMPLIFIED WAY, THE DIVERSE DEVELOPMENTS THAT TOOK PLACE IN THE WORLD OF design between the wars. It is, however, an apt title for the style that followed on immediately from Art Nouveau at the end of the nineteenth century. The latter had mostly relied on floral motifs to pattern and ornament its buildings and other artefacts, whereas Art Deco was thoroughly modern in turning away from the winding, sinuous qualities of Art Nouveau, looking instead to abstract design and colour for colour's sake. When turning to nature for inspiration, it preferred to portray animals, or the beauties of the female form.

While Art Deco upheld the importance of craftsmanship in response to the new mass production, it often benefited greatly from this development. Although Art Deco objects were originally made with rare and expensive materials, many ideas were copied and manufactured in cheaper alternatives. The movement started its life as a 'high style' and ended it as arguably the most populist and perhaps the most popular of all recognizable post-World War I styles. Art Deco style spread through every aspect of daily life between the wars; every form of art and craft adopted the new sensibility, whether it was the cinema, or the design for a radio set or motor car. Ultimately, the style fed on itself. At its most mundane, it became further and further removed from its origins in the decorative arts, especially with the use (or over use), distillation and repetition of its most durable decorative motifs, such as the fan, chevron and zigzag.

Where Art Nouveau had been heavy, complex and crowded, Art Deco was clean and pure. The lines in Art Deco did not swirl round like the centre of a whirlpool; if they curved, they were gradual and sweeping, following a fine arc; if they were straight, they were as straight as a ruler. Art Deco is not the opposite of Art Nouveau but in many ways an extension of it, particularly in its preoccupation with lavish ornamentation, fine materials and superlative craftsmanship.

ABOVE *Chryselephantine (bronze and ivory) statuary was a favoured Art Deco medium. 'Flame Leaper', a bronze, ivory and amber figure, is by Ferdinand Preiss, arguably the greatest chryselephantine sculptor of the period.*

LEFT *'The Comet' by Maurice Guiraud-Rivière, gilt and painted bronze allegorical female figure.*

ABOVE *The postcard, advertising a Manhattan shop selling Art Deco designs, is just one smart example of the enormous appeal of the 20s style to collectors today.*

RIGHT *Two-panel screen of lacquered wood by Léon Jallot.*

Art Deco could be light-hearted on one level and practical on another. As the style in a time of unprecedented change, it was fluid enough to reflect that change. It was the first truly twentieth century style; it was also to be the last total style. Like the Baroque, Classical or Regency styles, Art Deco could ornament a house, a yacht or a knife. Nothing has coloured and illuminated our life so extensively since.

Art Deco may have been the modern style, but it emerged from as many different sources as it had applications. Art Nouveau was of central importance to the rise of Art Deco, if only as a style to react against. Equally, the work of Hoffman, Olbrich, Peche, and Moser, who founded the Wiener Werkstätte at the beginning of the century, were early practitioners of a style which, when refined, looked like very early Art Deco. Another influence, which probably became the most important of all, was a response to primitive art. The impact of the Ballets Russes, whose stage designs and costumes mixed the oriental with the Westernized, the avant garde with the primitive, was also highly influential. Leon Bakst, its most famous designer, produced costumes whose lavishness and orientalism came as a complete shock to the Parisian public. Diaghilev's production of *Scheherezade* was a riot of deep, rich colour which inspired the heavier decorative side of Art Deco and interior design.

If oriental art had been made fashionable by the Ballets Russes, Mexican, Egyptian, North American Indian and South American art was of equal importance. The Egyptian influence, and also that of Africa, are obvious in the chairs of Pierre Legrain. Heavy, solid pieces of furniture, they are crude and built to last, much like the early radio sets and triangular clocks for the mantelpiece that instantly recall Egyptian pyramids or Aztec temples. What Art Deco learnt, and taught the public, was bold design. If colours were to be bright, they should knock you over, if lines were to be clear, they should be as stark and severe as the steps up to a temple. The obvious could be chic.

The final, and one of the most obvious, influences on Art Deco was there to see at every street corner, in every house, factory and shop, on the sea and in the air. The twentieth century was the Machine Age. Art Deco was modern because it used aspects of machine design as inspiration, the wings of an aeroplane, the bow of a yacht, the porthole of the cabin window of the new ocean liners, the

BELOW *The lure of pharaonic Egypt was strong in the Art Deco era, boosted by the discovery in 1922 of Tutankhamen's tomb. In the Egyptian taste is this stunning winged scarab brooch of 1924 by Cartier, the body of engraved smoked quartz, the wings of faïence and diamonds, both dotted with cabochon emeralds.*

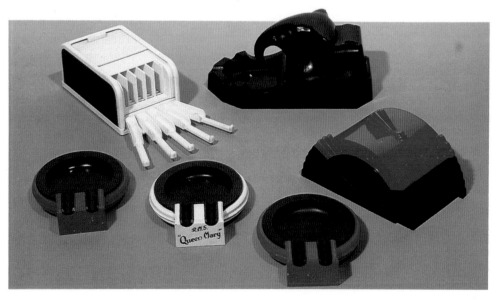

LEFT *Art Deco adopted new materials such as plastic, Bakelite and chrome with enthusiasm, as this selection of objects demonstrates. At the back are an open-and-close cigarette dispenser, an inkwell and a two-piece box featuring the favourite fan-edge motif. The three ashtrays in the foreground were all designed specifically for use on the luxury liner the R.M.S. Queen Mary.*

Design by
Leon Bakst for
Schéhérazade, probably
executed after the first
Paris production of
1910. The rich colour
and riot of pattern
characteristic of Bakst's
designs had considerable
influence on the
development of Art
Deco style.

cogs and wheels of a sewing machine or a motor car engine. It was even more modern because it accelerated the adoption of new materials such as plastic, Bakelite and chrome.

The mixing of all these influences made Art Deco the style it is. In the hands of genius, the objects transcended their sources. In the hands of competent designers, or plagiarists, they might become drab or garish, but they were, nevertheless, truly Art Deco.

It is impossible to talk of one Art Deco: there were as many directions, hybrids and strains as there were practitioners. Two extremes are identifiable, the exaggerated 'high Art Deco' of the French designers – Emile-Jacques Ruhlmann, Jean Dunand, Armand-Albert Rateau, Süe et Mare, René Lalique – versus the streamlined 'Moderne' style which was to become Modernism. At its most opulent, 'high style' Art Deco is distinguished by a lavish use of largely added decoration. In furniture this could take the form of veneers of exotic woods, inlays of mother-of-pearl, snakeskin or sharkskin coverings, layers of oriental lacquer, or applied-bronze mounts. The work of such Parisian artists as the furniture designer Armand-Albert Rateau or the cabinetmaker Emile-Jacques Ruhlmann is highly indicative of the extravagant and luxurious end of Art Deco craftsmanship in the 1920s and 1930s. In contrast, 'Moderne' design combines Art Deco motifs with streamform styling and modernistic geometrical configurations and decoration.

Not surprisingly, 'high' Art Deco is more concerned with expensive, luxurious objects with high production values and costs, intended for a fashionable and discerning clientele. The underlit mascots designed in glass for car radiators by René Lalique were obviously not intended to sit upon the Ford Model 'T'.

Motifs originally associated with 'high' Art Deco pieces eventually found their way – in however stylized and distilled a form – into the more public domain. For example, the Odeon Cinema in London's Leicester Square, was a testament to both the power of fashion and the lure of the new in the 1920s and 30s. Indeed, such cinema designs probably assisted greatly in the dissemination of the stylistic language which has come to be known as Art Deco.

Art Deco moved from the arena of high fashion into the workaday world, bringing

RIGHT *An example of Art Deco wit: millefiori-coloured cigarette case in cellulose nitrate, with a novelty clasp in the form of a hand.*

with it the values and the looks associated with high living, a fat bank balance and an opulence which could be set against the world's economic depression. The spread of the style has been described as a reaction to the austerity and deprivation occasioned by World War I; if this is the case, it is not surprising to find the echo of the luxury of the Art Deco motif in places of public entertainment as well as in the sunray gates, front doors and windows of the British suburban semi-detached house. At its most popular level, Art Deco was a symbol for a new postwar age, an age which was able to outlive the economic and political upheavals still to come. The style could only achieve this by being assimilated into a broader and more popular aesthetic, a process which was aided and encouraged in many different ways.

ARMAND-ALBERT RATEAU

Some of the most original – even whimsical – furniture being produced in Art Deco Paris was designed by Armand-Albert Rateau. His distinctive largely patinated-bronze and solid-oak pieces are inspired by the Orient and antiquity. The exotic bronze chair (right) with its leopard-skin cushion, features marine motifs – scallop shells at the top and

along the back, and tentacle-like legs. The bizarre patinated-bronze and marble table (below), c 1924, has four encrusted stylized birds as supports.

The elegance and opulence of Parisian Art Deco were best expressed in the stunning interiors of the 1920s and 30s, often the products of collaboration between furniture and textile designers, sculptors, painters, lacquer-workers and numerous other talented artists and artisans. The *ensemblier* came to the fore, with such names as Emile-Jacques Ruhlmann, Robert Mallet-Stevens, Francis Jourdain, Eileen Gray, and the partnership of Louis Süe and André Mare taking on the rather formidable task of creating a total design, or *ensemble*, for a room, including its wall, window and floor coverings, furniture and other accessories.

Art Deco designers often paid homage to the rich heritage of the Louis XV, Louis XVI and Empire periods, as well as creating entirely new forms of their own. They used both innovative and traditional materials, although their techniques were generally subsidiary to the overall aesthetic effect. Colours were often bright and vibrant, but subtle pastel shades and deep, dark greys, browns and blacks were also in evidence. The high style Art Deco interior and furnishings in Paris were above all luxuriant and lavish, with wealthy clients such as the couturiers Jacques Doucet, Jeanne Lanvin and Madeleine Vionnet commissioning furniture, *objets* and indeed whole rooms from the great designers.

High style designers were attracted by the unusual and exotic materials obtainable from the French colonies. They embellished and sometimes even entirely covered furniture with such exotic materials as mother-of-pearl, sharkskin (also known as shagreen or, in French, *galuchat*), snakeskin, gold and silver leaf, crushed eggshell lacquer, macassar ebony and ivory. These might form a pattern – usually stylized flowers or a geometric motif – or they might take advantage of the nature of the substance itself, perhaps using the imbricated pattern of the sharkskin decoratively. Oriental decorative techniques such as chinoiserie and lacquerwork were often an inspiration.

Expensive and élitist as the luxury trade undoubtedly was, its resurgence depended on other factors. Apart from a few specialist shops, the outlet for contemporary furniture was limited. When the new department stores realized that design could be of great use to them, the situation altered. Specialist outlets, such as the Studio Primavera, Studium Louvre, Pomone, and La Maîtrise, were established to provide the most modern furniture at a reasonable price. A further advantage of the studio system was that craftsmen were also allowed to accept private customers, where this did not interfere with the studio's work. Indeed, the furniture industry had a surprisingly liberal attitude, and skills were generously shared.

ABOVE *Lacquer and ivory screen depicting a snake and a panther, executed by Jean Dunand from a design by Paul Jouve.*

THE SUNBURST MOTIF

Of the geometric patterns beloved by Art Deco designers, the sunburst motif – whether partial, half or whole – is perhaps most ubiquitous, employed on a range of creations including furniture, jewellery, stained-glass windows and mass-produced biscuit tins.

TOP *These powder compacts reproduce Art Deco style in a range accessible to the less wealthy. With their sunburst patterns and apparently precious materials, they are in fact produced in inexpensive enamelled- and paste-encrusted metal.*

CENTRE LEFT *Archetypal Art Deco luxury: a chair of ebony, ivory and sharkskin designed by Clément Rousseau, signed and dated 1921.*

CENTRE RIGHT *A full, glorious sunburst fills the rock crystal, ruby and diamond brooch of c 1925.*

BOTTOM LEFT *Kid shoes with an asymmetric sunburst design by Pinet, 1930s.*

BOTTOM RIGHT *English talcum-powder bottle sporting a quarter-sunburst pattern.*

The greatest *ébéniste*, or cabinetmaker, of French Art Deco, was perhaps Emile-Jacques Ruhlmann (1879–1933). He produced forms which were simple and elegant, usually traditional in shape and technique, but sleekly modern in decoration and detail. His desks, cabinets, tables and chairs were veneered in costly, warm woods, such as amaranth, amboyna, ebony and violet wood, and embellished with silk tassels and subtle touches of ivory in dentate, dotted or diamond patterns. The long, slender legs – sometimes torpedo-shaped with cut facets – were often capped with metal sabots, or shoes, a concept that was both decorative and practical. Ruhlmann was also the supreme *ensemblier*, designing rugs, fabrics, wallpapers and porcelain; he was a fine draughtsman as well, and in 1924 he published a book containing watercolours of his interiors and detailed studies of sketches which followed the stages of his design from conception to finished product.

Ruhlmann's furniture always allows for an uncomplicated appreciation of each material. The more eccentric style of Pierre Legrain (1887–1929), designer of the famous 'Zebra' chaise longue of 1925, is perhaps the antithesis of Ruhlmann's style. This piece of furniture appears almost intentionally perverse. The zebra skin is imitated in velvet, the armrest

BELOW *Emile-Jacques Ruhlmann was the best-known of all French Art Deco furniture designers. In the late 1920s and early 1930s his luxury furniture, made of the rarest materials, was based on French neo-Classical styles but later he experimented with slightly more modern materials and forms.*

which would conventionally be against a wall is expensively decorated on the reverse with abstract patterns in mother-of-pearl – the overall design is almost crude, exuding a feeling of gratuitous luxury and decadence.

Another equally eccentric furniture designer was Jean Dunand (1887–1942), known for his *dinanderie* (the art of chasing and hammering metal) and for his lacquerwork. He also designed and decorated elaborate furniture, including cabinets, panels and screens, often covered with figural or animal designs, either by Dunand himself or after a noted artist. His huge screens, often of silver, gold and black lacquer, displayed massive geometric motifs, exotic oriental or African maidens, lush landscapes or elaborate mythological scenes.

As well as the luxury productions of high style Art Deco, this period saw the early experiments in what we have now come to recognize as modern furniture, reacting against gratuitous ornament and using metals and plastics in forms which could lead to eventual mass production. Even such a master of high style as Ruhlmann was attracted to the use of chrome and silvered metal towards the end of his career, when many of his furniture forms became quite rectilinear. At the same time, his ivory dots and silk fringes gave way to chrome fittings, leather cushions and swivel bases.

ABOVE *Black lacquer desk by Jean Dunand and Serge Revinski, c1925. The hinged central writing slope is covered with lozenges of shagreen.*

LEFT *The famous 'Zebra' chaise longue in black lacquer by Pierre Legrain, 1925.*

Glass produced during the Art Deco period ranged from the serene, handblown vessels of Maurice Marinot in France and the delicately engraved Graal glass of the Swedes, Hald and Gate, to the perfume bottles of Baccarat and the tableware of America's Libbey Glass Company. In addition, massive panels of stained glass and *verre-églomisé* (glass painted on the reverse side) were produced for homes, churches and ocean liners.

In France, the two major names and influences were Maurice Marinot (1882 to 1960) and René Lalique (1860 to 1945). Marinot started and ended his working life as a painter, becoming a member of the renegade Fauve group, known for their wild and colourful canvases. But between 1911 and 1937, he devoted himself to the art of glassmaking. His most exemplary vases, jars and bottles – he produced some 2,500 in all – were thick-walled, stunning objects which elevated the medium of glass to new artistic heights. By emphasizing its actual physical qualities, by seeming miraculously to trap its fluidity in three dimensions, he produced pieces that captivated critics and public alike. What had hitherto been considered flaws in the medium – bubbles, specks of chemicals needed to produce colour and so on – he turned into primary decorative components. These elements, coupled with the traditional ovoid, spherical and squarish forms that so many Art Deco vessels assumed (metal and ceramic, as well as glass), resulted in some of the most beautiful *objets d'art* of the period. He also submerged pieces in acid baths to create deeply etched designs, and produced multilayered works with various colours or streaks contained within the separate layers.

René Lalique, who had had a successful earlier career as the premier Art Nouveau goldsmith was the undisputed *maître verrier*. Besides designing perfume bottles for Coty, D'Orsay, Worth and at least two dozen other *parfumeurs*, he produced countless boxes, figures (including automobile mascots), vases, clock and picture frames and tableware mostly in his own characteristic heavy glass, which had a luminous opalescent appearance. He also

THE FEMME FATALE

The perennial fascination of the female form attracted many Art Deco glassmakers, including Lalique, Descomps and Argy-Rousseau. Their model of feminine beauty was the 'dancer', who was invariably either partly or completely naked and could suggest the exotic, the mysterious, the femme fatale.

LEFT *This group of vases shows the range of colours, shapes and motifs found on the vessels of René Lalique.*

BELOW *A selection of etched glass vases and table lamps by Daum, 1920s. The enamelled glass is a typical of Daum's style during this period.*

LEFT *Flask and stopper, hand-blown and acid-etched by Maurice Marinot, 1929. Many of his works were internally decorated with air bubbles or chemical inclusions: within this piece float tiny black particles.*

created one-of-a-kind vessels in *cire-perdue* (lost wax) glass, as well as monumental architectural pieces, including figural panels for Claridge's hotel in London and John Wanamaker's department store in Philadelphia.

Other French glassmakers enthusiastically embraced Art Deco, including the esteemed Daum Frères which had produced Art Nouveau glass in the 1880s and 1890s in the naturalistic style of Emile Gallé. In the 1930s, the factory created etched-glass wares very much in the

contemporary vein, with geometric and stylized-floral patterns often reminiscent of Marinot's vessels, but usually more colourful and decorative. Charles Schneider, who occasionally designed for Daum, founded his own Cristallerie Schneider in 1913, and he became known for his *intercalaires*; coloured inclusions sandwiched between two layers of glass. His works were signed *Charder* (derived from his first and last names), *Le Verre Français* or, simply, *Schneider*.

The ancient Egyptian technique of *pâte-de-verre* had been revived by Henri Cros at the turn-of-the-century. This technique involves mixing powdered glass into a paste with water and a fluxing medium, then refiring it in a mould, producing a cold glass compound that can be modelled like clay and coloured easily. A number of Art Deco glassmakers continued to employ the process. Foremost among them was François-Emile Décorchement (1880–1971), who also produced near-transparent *pâte-de-cristal* vessels by using a higher percentage of lead. Many of his massive, thick-walled pieces were decorated with stylized floral or faunal motifs.

Gabriel Argy-Rousseau (1885–1953) also produced *pâte-de-verre* and *pâte-de-cristal* glass, manufacturing a wide range of decorative objects. These included small lamps and three-dimensional neo-Classical figures, usually of dancers, some modelled by sculptor Marcel Bouraine. Argy-Rousseau's vessels were less massive and more delicate than Décorchement's; indeed, floral and figural decorations on his early pieces were sometimes more reminiscent of Art Nouveau. However, the motifs he produced after World War I – stylized female heads, classical masks, elegant gazelles or floral forms – were more in keeping with 1920s French style. Alméric Walker was another *pâte-de-verre* designer whose career spanned the Art Nouveau and Art Deco periods. He collaborated with the sculptors Henri Bergé and Jean Descomps, and at one point he worked for Daum, producing an array of *pâte-de-verre* vases, ashtrays, bowls and statuettes. Most of his works are highly sculptural, decorated with frogs, lizards, goldfish and beetles rendered naturalistically. The most Art Deco of his creations are stunning figures of veiled women dancers in dramatic poses.

Some superb stained-glass works were produced in France in the Art Deco style, including windows and panels by Maurice Jallot, J. Gaudin, Gaétan Jeannin and Jacques Gruber, the last of whom had produced stunning Art Nouveau designs as well. A series of windows with sports players executed for the dining room of a resort hotel is particularly striking.

ABOVE *Jacques Gruber's earlier stained glass works were in the Art Nouveau style, but this window, one of a series of sports players executed for the dining room of a resort hotel, is pure Art Deco.*

Another supreme achievement in glass is the massive *verre-églomis* mural produced by Charles Champigneulle for the French liner *Normandie* to the design of Jean Dupas.

Other European countries, as well as the United States, produced Art Deco glass of merit, including the Leerdam company in Holland and the Orrefors company in Scandinavia. In England, the design and manufacture of glassware was never as inventive as that of the French, but what it lost in complexity, or colour, it made up for in simplicity. Where the English might engrave a glass with clear-cut lines, with the occasional ornamental motif, the French would burn or scour deep into the glass. Both were equally viable, and are good examples of the fluid diversity of the Art Deco style, and of the new techniques available to designers in glass.

RIGHT *'The Negro Hut',*
blown- and engraved-
glass piece designed by
Edvard Hald for the
Scandinavian Orrefors
Company, 1918.
Tribal art was one of
the inspirations of Art
Deco, as this piece
shows.

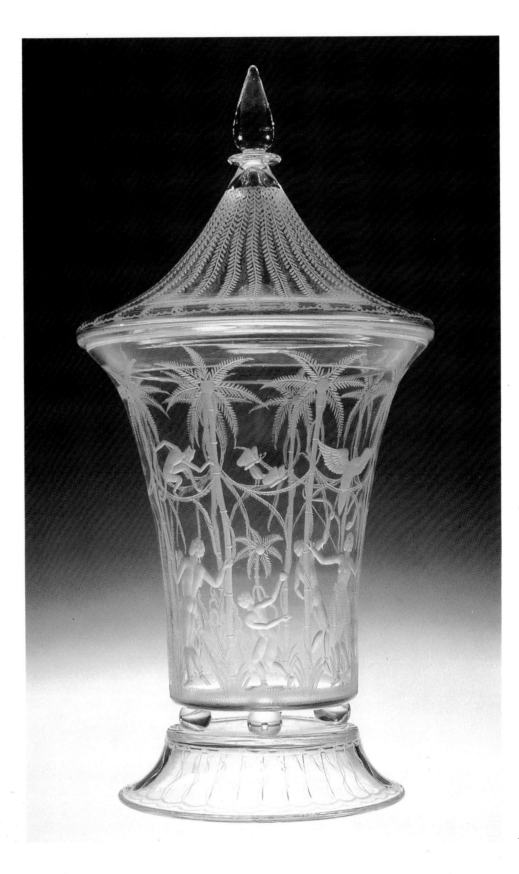

Of all the applications of Art Deco, the medium of ceramics was without doubt the most widespread: even the arrival of materials such as plastics, Bakelite and phenolic resin did not detract from its popularity or commercial success. Art Deco ceramics provided the style with a huge boost, because they were attractive and readily available. More often than not, the basic shape of plates, vases, cups and saucers was left alone. The undecorated object could then be used like an artist's canvas, and novel decorations could be painted or stencilled on. Some craftsmen experimented with irregularly shaped vessels – zig-zagged vases and sugar bowls or cups with triangular (and hard to grasp) handles. Art Deco ceramics could also take the form of ebullient, sensuous or humorous figures: dancing couples in vivid costumes, earthenware female busts with corkscrew curls, smiling pigs with purple spots.

Geometry was a keyword in Art Deco ceramics, from the ovals and orbs dominating the shapes of French glazed stoneware to the triangles and circles decorating pots in England, the United States, Germany and even Russia. But added to a rigid geometric form, there could be a stylized floral design, a frieze of deer – the popular 'biches' motif – or great swirls of bright colour.

The most serene and classical ceramics of the period emanated from France. Emile Decoeur (1876-1953) worked in faïence, stoneware and porcelain. Before 1920 his vessels were generally decorated with geometric or floral designs which later gave way to heavy, pale-coloured glazes, sometimes mottled, sometimes tinged with darker hues at the rim, but always applied to traditionally shaped vessels. Emile Lenoble (1875–1940), on the other hand, almost always decorated his classical forms with floral and abstract designs, as well as with coloured *craquelure* glazes. His stylized motifs could be moulded in a subtle bas-relief, incised in the applied slip or clay, or painted over or under the glaze.

Mass-produced tableware in both porcelain and earthenware, with handsome Art Deco motifs, also emerged from France. Among the designers were Suzanne Lalique, (René's daughter), Marcel Goupy and Jean Luce. Established factories such as Sèvres produced Art Deco porcelain, including elegant vases with stylized floral designs and monumental display pieces.

In England, Clarice Cliff and Susie Cooper produced exuberant and colourful designs quite antithetical to those of France. Clarice Cliff (1899–1972), with her bold, lively colours and patterns, was probably Britain's best-known

BELOW *Dancing couple, part of the 'Age of Jazz' series by Clarice Cliff.*

LEFT *The best-known name in Art Deco ceramics is that of Clarice Cliff, the Staffordshire-born designer whose brightly hued tableware has come to be considered by many as the greatest manifestation of the Art Deco style in the UK. Her distinctive glazes and designs are what she is best known for, and these were often bright, bold patterns influenced by the designs of Diaghilev's Ballets Russes.*

ceramics designer. Her most famous designs were the 'Bizarre' range of tableware, introduced in 1928. The pieces bore strong, simple designs – flowers, landscapes, geometric patterns – in bright hues, including vivid colours quite new to British ceramics, such as purple and a shade of orange she called 'tango'. She also decorated limited-edition pieces; among her most distinctively Art Deco was a series of ceramic cut-out figures known as the 'Age of Jazz' featuring black-tie-clad musicians and dancing couples. During her career, she hired well-known artists and sculptors – including Graham Sutherland, Ben Nicholson, Barbara Hepworth, Paul Nash and the Bloomsbury artists Duncan Grant and Vanessa Bell – to work on designs that she then manufactured.

Fashion played an important role in Art

THE *BICHES* MOTIF

Deer, gazelles, elands, stags and various other biches ('does'), as they were collectively called, appeared on a wide variety of Art Deco objects, their inherent elegance lending itself to creative interpretation.

Deco design, not only in terms of its direct influence on other media – the Ballets Russes costumes, for instance, made waves – but also because many of its leading lights, Paul Poiret, Jacques Doucet and Jeanne Lanvin among them, were extraordinary collectors and taste-makers who helped enormously to promote *Le Style 25*.

Fashion illustration was significant as well; not only did the drawings of Paul Iribe, Georges Lepape, George Barbier and Erté help in themselves to spread the new couture, but their styles and use of vivid colours had a strong influence on many other artists in France and elsewhere.

Fashion accessories – handbags, powder compacts, fans, cigarette cases – were designed in abundance in the 1920s and 1930s, often with bold geometric and floral motifs that were every bit as masterful as those decorating furniture, ceramics and textiles. Jewellery, too, reflected the spirit of Modernism, whether made of precious stones and metals – by Cartier, Tiffany or Van Cleef & Arpels – or of lesser materials such as glass, plastic, paste and base metal, sometimes by anonymous designers, sometimes by those as renowned as René Lalique.

In Parisian fashion design, as in other media, the influence of the Ballets Russes was paramount. At the same time the impact of Paul Poiret (1879–1944) was being felt, with his fluid dress designs distinguished by their smooth, corset-less line. In 1908, Paul Iribe's vividly coloured *pochoirs* (stencilled ink drawings) illustrating his new fashions, heralded a new era, not only in design but in illustration as well. Preceding most of Art Deco by at least a decade, they were very much in the forefront of the style. The great early Paris couturiers were to bring fashion dramatically to the fore, making it as influential as any other design medium, a circumstance that has remained a constant in following decades.

Jewellery and accessories in the Art Deco period were as varied and colourful as the fashions themselves. Great French goldsmiths fashioned miniature works of art in platinum, gold, diamonds, emeralds and other precious

ABOVE *Some of Art Deco's boldest geometric designs in jewellery were produced by the Parisian Raymond Templier. This handsome bracelet, c1925–30, is not only a chic, streamlined essay on the circle and the square, but a* tour de force *of ingenuity as well: the central panel, of platinum, white gold, onyx and diamonds, can be removed and worn as a brooch. The wide bracelet itself is of silver.*

LE DÉPART POUR LE CASINO
MANTEAU DU SOIR, DE WORTH

Nº 1 de la Gazette.   Modèle déposé. Reproduction interdite.   Année 1923. — Planche 1

ABOVE *Coloured fashion plates abounded in the Art Deco period, promoting contemporary couture as well as shaping modern illustration. George Barbier's 1923 drawing for an evening coat by Worth appeared in* La Gazette du Bon Ton, *an influential Parisian journal and depicts a chic couple bound for the casino.*

LEFT *Art Deco handbags and shoes speak of an era of high quality, and expensive accessories.*

gems – some starkly geometric, others with Egyptian or oriental overtones, still others wildly florid and encrusted with stones of many colours. Such hardstones as onyx, turquoise, jade and lapis lazuli were also used, and enamelling was widely applied.

Unlike Art Nouveau jewellery, which often involved realistic floral, figural or faunal motifs. Art Deco tended to be simpler; it was usually either geometric or abstract, and even when it featured flowers or other realistic elements, was quite subtle and underplayed. The fashions of the day – cloche hats, short hair, short hemlines, short sleeves – demanded complementary jewellery forms. Brooches were worn on hat brims, on shoulders, on hips, on belts; long strands of beads, or *sautoirs*, hung from the neck; bracelets and bangles of all kinds adorned the arm, and dangling earrings and small ear clips appeared in myriad handsome guises. In addition, both fancy wrist and pendant watches appeared, while powder compacts and cigarette cases became *de rigueur* for the bold woman of fashion. Inexpensive versions of all these items were fashioned of paste, plastic and base metal. The application of coloured enamel to the metal pieces often made them, despite being cheap and mass-produced, every bit as handsome as the more expensive models.

As with furniture, the use of exotic new materials was promoted as jewellery ceased to be limited to traditional precious stones and metals. The adoption of platinum as a setting enabled jewellers to accentuate the other elements. Platinum is far stronger than gold or silver, and the settings for stones could therefore be much reduced. Other new materials were: onyx, ebony, chrome, plastic, lacquered metals, agate, coral, Bakelite, rhinestones, jade, tortoiseshell, jet and moonstone. Used in conjunction, these materials offered up a riot of colour and contrasting textures.

LEFT *The opulent decoration of New York's Chanin Building was not merely external. This is the Executive Suite bathroom; its decoration, like that of the entire building, was supervised by Jacques Delamarre. Characteristcally Art Deco is the sunburst pattern over the engraved-glass shower doors; note also the row of avian tiles near the ceiling, which hide a ventilating duct.*

RIGHT *Elevator door of the Chrysler Building, by William van Alen, the most characteristically Art Deco of the New York skyscrapers.*

The most important legacy of the Arts and Crafts Movement for Art Deco was the concept of collaboration between craftsmen. The heroic example of the Renaissance Man who could turn his hand to anything had been replaced by specialization in particular trades and crafts. At the turn-of-the-century, there were two men who singlehandedly proved themselves exceptions to the rule. The American, Frank Lloyd Wright, and Josef Hoffman, an Austrian, were geniuses, giants in the history of architecture and design. Both proved to be invaluable examples of and fore-runners of the Art Deco style. Frank Lloyd Wright's massive project for the Midway Gardens in Chicago,

contemporary with the zenith of the Art Deco style, and his 1912 designs for the Avery Coonery Playhouse in Chicago, Illinois, are well ahead of their time. Hoffman's Palais Stoclet in Belgium shows a similar attention to detail while still maintaining a sense of the whole. Their work was extraordinary, visionary but, particularly for the Art Deco movement, almost impossible to emulate.

The introduction of new materials brought new problems, and the search for a new style demanded a new approach to the large commission or project. What was needed was cooperation between all the mastercraftsmen. The example of Modernism which stressed a need to reappraise all given ideas, promoted an atmosphere in which interchange between different disciplines was encouraged and promoted. Why bother to learn to weld, inlay wood, work with lacquer, bend chrome, blow glass, mould plastics, cast Bakelite, when all you needed to do was seek out the relevant craftsman? Art Deco was revolutionary in that it promoted the concept of the designer. The designer could be at worst a dilettante or mediocre amateur, at best a brilliant innovator and promoter of the possibilities created by other people's expertise.

Although Art Deco is best-known to us through its smaller objects, such as posters, textiles and ceramics, it is the large commissions which display the full possibilities of the style. The Exposition des Arts Décoratifs et Industriels, the magnificent French ocean liner, the *Normandie*, the glass entrance to the Strand Palace Hotel, now in the Victoria and Albert Museum, London, the preserved splendours of the ballroom in London's Park Lane Hotel, and New York's Radio City Music Hall, or the stylized elegance of the Hoover factory in England, marooned on the A40 London to Oxford road or, more spectacularly, the dizzying, skyscraping summit of the Chrysler building are just some examples of Art Deco at its most ambitious and successful.

LEFT *Main lobby, Union Trust Building, Detroit, 1929. The lobby has a distinctly ecclesiastical flavour, in keeping with the building's sobriquet, 'Cathedral of Finance'. The vast vaulted ceiling features bright Rookwood tiles: imported travertine marble columns, Mankato stone, Belgian black marble and red Numidian marble compound a kaleidoscope effect further set off by glistening metal doors, cashier desks and trim.*

In the early 1930s, the ship *Normandie* was to provide a splendid opportunity for French craftsmen. Run by La Compaignie Générale Transatlantique, the *Normandie* project enjoyed the sponsorship of a government which had wisely recognized that a floating showcase of the decorative arts would enhance French prestige abroad. The scale of the liner and the massive investment in it allowed for an unrivalled decorative commission, and the list of craftsmen who worked on various aspects of the *Normandie* reads like a catalogue of the cream of Art Deco. Tragically, this splendour was to be short-lived. In 1941 the ship was commandeered by the United States government as a troop carrier, and while being modified for this purpose a workman accidentally set fire to the ship that was boasted to be 100 percent fireproof. Most of the greatest works of Art Deco ended up at the bottom of New York harbour.

No detail was omitted to make this 'floating palace' the most luxurious liner yet conceived. Tableware in glass, porcelain and silver was commissioned from such craftsmen as master silversmith Jean Puiforcat. At least three of France's greatest specialists in metalwork were employed on the commission: Adelbert Szabo, Edgar Brandt and Raymond Henri Subes. Szabo created doors for the first-class dining room, and Brandt was also commissioned to design doors and gates. Subes, who worked both in wrought iron and later in steel lacquered in Duco varnish, was, in collaboration with the architects Patout and Paçon, one of the few artists to display his designs for elements of the *Normandie* at the Salons des Artistes Décorateurs in 1933 and 1935, also in Paris.

The *tour de force* was the grand salon, dominated by the four panels – each measuring 50 by 22ft (15¾ by 6¾m) – produced by Charles Champignuelle to the design of Jean Dupas. The technique of *verre-églomisé* employed involved painting on the reverse side of plate-glass panels, which were then highlighted with gold and silver leaf and finally affixed to a canvas backing. The panels depict the history of navigation in fantastic splendour, complete with a Moses-like Neptune riding on a sea serpent, muscular steeds and mermen, a flock of seagulls and glittering galleons, all floating and flying on a background of stylized waves. Sadly, only one panel survives today, which may be seen at the Metropolitan Museum in New York. Against a background of theatrical splendour, with Dupas's panels and Jean Beaumont's 20ft (6m) lengths of curtain decorated with cerise wisteria on a cream ground, were hundreds of abundantly stuffed chairs and canopies designed by F. Gaudissart and upholstered by Aubusson in tapestry woven with flowers from various French colonies. The lavish ivory and olive tones on vivid orange-red and grey grounds, set against the gold and silver leaf of the murals, produced an unrivalled image of splendour.

The abundant publicity given to the project must have given those who had neither the money nor the desire to travel on the *Normandie* an idea of the style and chic aboard the liner. The influence of the *Normandie* commission was to spread through all branches of the decorative arts.

RIGHT *'Dawn', 32-panel wall decoration for the Grand Salon of the* Normandie *in gessoed wood by Jean Dunand and Jean Dupas.*

RIGHT *These panels, showing the top of a golden galleon, were once part of the great* History of Navigation *panel in the Grand Salon of the* Normandie.

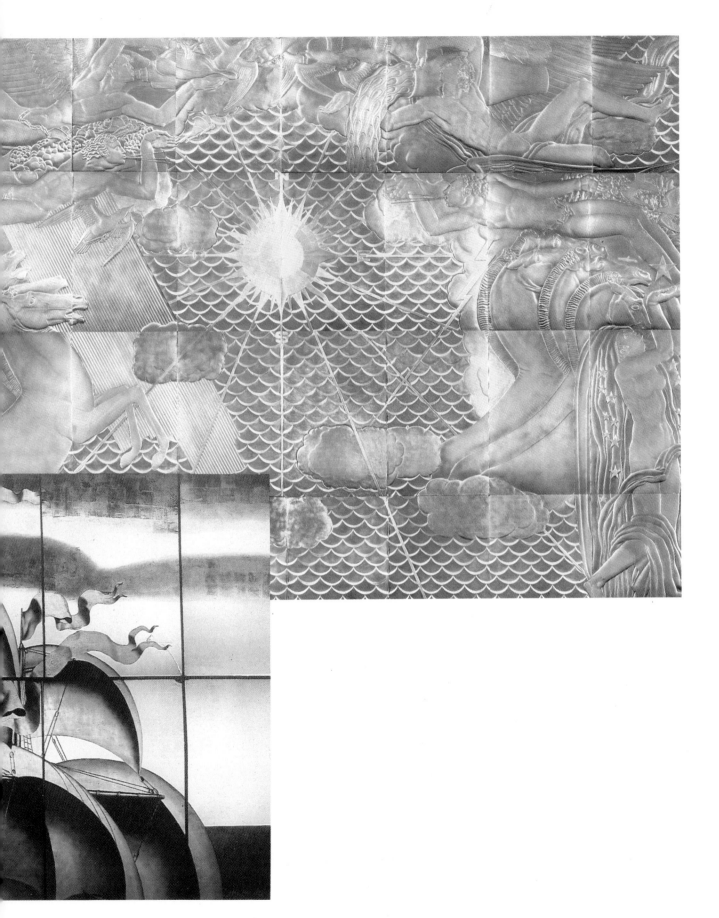

4. MODERN*ism*

FROM THE VERY START ART DECO HAD COMPRISED TWO EXTREMES OF STYLE. ON THE ONE HAND, IN FRANCE where the movement evolved, and notably in Paris, high style Art Deco manifested itself emotionally, with exuberance, colour and playfulness. On the other hand, elsewhere in Europe, and later in the United States, it was given a more intellectual interpretation based on theories of functionalism and economy, and this element of design, known today as Modernism, merits a chapter in its own right. Though both share a twentieth-century preoccupation with contemporary sources and inspiration, the ultimate limitations of Art Deco prevented further developments, while Modernism was to lead to new directions.

By 1926, the loosely knit band of French Modernists – Francis Jordain, Pierre Chareau, Le Corbusier, Robert Mallet-Stevens and René Herbst – had become increasingly outspoken in their criticism of the Art Deco designers who catered to select clients by creating elaborately crafted *pièces uniques*, or limited editions. The Modernists argued that the new age required nothing less than excellent design for everyone, and that quality and mass-production were not mutually exclusive: an object's greatest beauty lay in its perfect adaptation to its usage. Each age must create a decorative style to meet its specific needs, and in the late 1920s this aim was best realized by industry's newest means of production, the machine. Existing concepts of beauty, based on the artisan and his hand tools, thus needed to be redefined to meet the dictates of the new Machine Age.

Modernism made rapid progress in the late 1920s, although most designers took a stance somewhat short of the severe functionalism espoused by its most ardent adherents. As Paul Follot, a veteran designer, observed in 1928: 'We know that the 'necessary' alone is not sufficient for man and that the superfluous is indispensable for him . . . or otherwise let us also suppress music, flowers, perfumes . . . and the smiles of ladies!' Follot's viewpoint was shared by most of his designer colleagues – even if logic called for the immediate elimin-

RIGHT *Housing scheme, Hook of Holland, by J. J. P. Oud, 1924–27. This scheme comprised two terraces of cheap housing with shops at the end of each block. The apparent simplicity of the houses with their white-painted rendered façades and horizontal bands of windows looks forward to the full-blown International Style.*

ation of all ornamentation, humankind was not psychologically prepared for such an abrupt dislocation in lifestyle. Most designers therefore opted for a middle ground, creating machine-made items that retained an element of decoration – which, ironically, often had to be hand-finished.

Outside France, functionalism had a longer history, having dominated decorative-arts ideology since the end of the Victorian era. In Munich, the formation of the Deutscher Werkbund in 1907 carried forward the logic and geometry at the heart of the Vienna Secession and Glasgow movements some years

earlier. In contrast to both the French Art Nouveau repertoire of flowers and maidens and Germany's own lingering Jugendstil, the Werkbund placed emphasis on functional designs which could be mass-produced. A reconciliation between art and industry, updated to accommodate the technological advances of the new century, was implemented, with ornament given only secondary status. These ideals were realized more fully with the formation of the Bauhaus in Germany, which in turn inspired the Modernist strain that took root in American decorative arts in the late 1920s. After World War I many Euro-

pean and Scandinavian designers followed the German example by creating Bauhaus-inspired furnishings and objects.

In Holland, the De Stijl (the name means 'Style') group of architects and designers, who issued their first manifesto in November 1918, were to play an important part in the development of Modernism. They believe that art, architecture and design should aspire to universality rather than to individuality, and that a universal 'style' was emerging, that would both symbolize and precipitate universal harmony.

The De Stijl belief that progress and perfection, on both a material and metaphysical level, could be demonstrated by means of the new formal and spatial harmonies made possible by the use of materials such as steel, concrete and glass, was of course, shared by designers and architects in France, Germany and Russia, and van Doesburg travelled widely throughout Europe in the 1920s, exchanging ideas with other like-minded theorists. By 1925, for example, De Stijl had an international membership, van Doesburg having recruited campaigners from Russia, Austria and the Bauhaus.

The most remarkable and influential of the De Stijl designers, however, was Gerrit Rietveld (1888–1964), a carpenter by training, who studied architecture in evening classes and who designed two of the most famous 'icons' of the Modern Movement: the Red-Blue chair in 1917, and the Schroeder house in Utrecht in 1924.

Rietveld, who was the son of a cabinetmaker, set up his own furniture workshop in 1911; his early work is simple and carefully handcrafted, in keeping with the Dutch Arts and Crafts tradition. In 1916, however, he was introduced first to the painter Bart van der Leck, at that time a member of the De Stijl group, and then to the architect Robert van t'Hoff, who asked him to copy, from photographs, furniture by Frank Lloyd Wright for the *Huis ter Heide* (1916). The Red-Blue chair was designed a few months after this, its formal and spatial innovations no doubt inspired by Rietveld's recent encounters with new attitudes to materials and form. The chair was, in fact, designed as a personal experiment to demonstrate that 'a thing of beauty, eg a spatial object, could be made of nothing but straight machined materials.' Following its illustration in *De Stijl* magazine, however, it became widely known in avant-garde circles throughout Europe.

In much the same way, Rietveld built his famous Schröder House as an exercise in three-dimensional planar composition, with colour picking out the architectural detail. Influenced by Wright's use of asymmetrical plans in his Prairie Style houses, the Schröder House appears to be constructed out of over-

lapping and intersecting two-dimensional planes that enclose three-dimensional space. The white and grey walls of the exterior are cut and highlighted by the graphic lines of the balcony railings and by the window mullions painted red, blue, yellow and black. The distribution of wall to window space is approximately equal, so that the solidity of construction is undermined by the sheer volume of openings. By abolishing all the traditional signs by which a building is 'read' and understood – symmetry, a fixed plan, obvious load-bearing supports – Rietveld created a blueprint with seemingly endless possibilities.

ABOVE *The Schröder House, Utrecht, by Gerrit Rietveld, 1923–4. Rietveld used a lightweight steel frame for this house so that the walls were no longer weight-bearing, enabling him to position internal walls where desired rather than where necessary. Panels of reinforced concrete were used to create balconies and overhangs.*

GERRIT RIETVELD CHAIRS

Gerrit Rietveld started his own cabinet-making business in 1911, continually experimenting with designs. He produced his famous Red-Blue Chair (left) about 1918. The Berlin Chair (far left) of 1923 is in some ways an even more exaggerated demonstration of belief in the principles of De Stijl: it is much simpler, and uses only tones of black-and-white. In 1927 Rietveld designed the Beugel Fauteuil (below left), which appears to resemble the Red-Blue Chair in plywood and tube, but in fact takes its strength from the integral triangles from which it is formed. Rietveld produced an extraordinary variety of innovative chair designs, typically planned with mass production in mind. His concern for the method as well as the result of design led to the Birza Chair (left), cut from a single piece of fibre which was then folded and fixed into a rigid shape

Of all the major manufacturing countries, it was Germany that was perhaps best prepared for the functional and machine-friendly approach of Modernism. Although the machine-versus-craftsman debate was carried on as vociferously as elsewhere, German artists were amongst the first to seek the answer in a synthesis of the two rather than in a rejection of mechanized production. A typical German interpretation of the English Arts and Crafts Movement was that of Hermann Muthesius, one of the most influential architects and designers in the pre-Bauhaus era. He argued for the industrialization of design: 'Let the human mind think of shapes the machine can produce,' he wrote in *Das Englische Haus* (1904–5). 'Such shapes, once they are logically developed in accordance with what machines can do, we may certainly call artistic. They will satisfy because they will no longer be imitation handicrafts but typical machine-made shapes.'

As early as 1907, with the establishment of the Deutscher Werkbund by a number of Secessionist designers, German designers were aiming to improve the quality of manufactured goods and promote the role of designers in industry. Amongst the designers involved in the Werkbund was the Belgian Henri van de Velde, who set up a school of arts and crafts in Weimar. This school was to provide the premises and some of the staff for the Bauhaus, which was to be one of the major influences in Modernism.

Walter Gropius (1883–1969) was chosen as director from a list supplied by van de Velde. His appointment was confirmed in 1919, and in that year the school officially changed its name to the Staatliches Bauhaus im Weimar ('Weimar State Architectural Institute'). In his opening proclamation, Gropius urged the breaking down of barriers between artists and craftsmen, at the same time stating unequivocally the principle of the *Gesamtkunstwerk* which was to be the Bauhaus goal: 'The ultimate aim of all visual arts is the complete building . . . Architects, painters and sculptors must recognize anew and learn to grasp the composite character of a building both as an entity and its separate parts.'

The Bauhaus was set up as a series of workshops and in its initial form was inspired by an admiration for the British Arts and Crafts Movement. All students had to take a generalized *Vorkurs*, which covered the characteristics of materials and the processes of arts and crafts: in many ways it was a prototype for the foundation course taken by many art students today. After completing this basic course, students could proceed to the craft workshop of their choice.

BELOW *Woven silk tapestry made by Anni Albers at the Bauhaus weaving workshop, 1926.*

ABOVE *Fagus Works,
Alfeld-an-der-Leine, by
Walter Gropius, 1911.
One of the first truly
modern buildings, the
Fagus Works was
essentially a cubic block
incorporating glass
curtain-walling that
extended around the
corners with no need for
additional support.*

RIGHT *Stoneware bottle
designed by Gerhard
Marcks and executed by
Max Krehan at the
Bauhaus pottery
workshop at Dornburg,
c1922.*

In 1923 the Bauhaus staged its first important exhibition, at which the central exhibit was an experimental house designed by the painter Georg Muche. The Haus am Horn was one of the first prototypes for a house that could be made from mass-produced components: the prevailing spirit was of functionalism, with each room built to fulfil a single purpose, and Marcel Breuer's kitchen was especially prophetic, making use of a continuous work surface with cupboards suspended above and below. The exhibition was well received: Walter Passarge, in *Das Kunstblatt*, wrote of 'Very beautiful textiles, ceramics, and metalwork . . . in all these works, one perceives the thorough training in craftsmanship.' However, it was not art critics which the Bauhaus had to attract, but the leaders of industry.

In 1925, growing nationalist hostility forced the Bauhaus to leave Weimar. Gropius found a new location in the industrial city of Dessau, where the Bauhaus entered a mature, post-experimental phase, geared towards the training of all industrial designers and the production of designs that were first of all practical. Where the products of the Weimar Bauhaus had been essentially individualistic, handmade crafts not suitable for mass production, the Dessau Bauhaus adopted a more practical stance. There is a new air of reality about Gropius's *Principles of Bauhaus Production* published in 1926: 'The products reproduced from prototypes that have been developed by the Bauhaus can be offered at a reasonable price only by utilization of all the modern, economical methods of standardization (mass production by industry) and by large scale sales.'

At Dessau, the workshops were subjected to a thorough reorganization. Ceramics, woodwork, stained glass and bookbinding were dropped, and in 1929 the stage workshop ceased to exist. In 1927 a new architecture department was established. Despite the Bauhaus's recognition of the supreme importance of this field, previously architecture had not been studied in its own right. In 1929 a new Photography Workshop was introduced. After 1928, the cabinetmaking and metal workshops were amalgamated into the new Department of Interior Design; the sculpture workshop became the Plastic Workshop, while the printing workshop was renamed the Printing and Advertising Department. The weaving workshop, which had been one of the few commercially successful departments at Weimar, continued at Dessau with the same staff.

ABOVE *Bauhaus Workshops by Walter Gropius, 1925–6. Here the curtain-wall is at last fully developed, and forms a transparent screen, completely exposing the structure within.*

ABOVE *Bauhaus glass, designed by Josef Albers. After the school had moved from Weimar to Dessau, Albers ran the Department of Interior Design with Alfred Arndt.*

RIGHT *The Wassily Chair by Marcel Breuer, 1925. This chair, has been in continual production since 1925. Its historical importance in generating the designs of Mart Stam and Mies van der Rohe is undeniable.*

Although the Weimar Bauhaus had had some success, notably with furniture, typography and textiles, the Dessau Bauhaus proved far more commercially minded and enjoyed even greater acclaim. Its most notable achievements were a wide range of light fixture designs, including the Kandem range of desk lamps, and also textiles, both woven and printed, and wallpapers. The first wallpapers were not produced commercially until 1929, but thereafter proved one of the Bauhaus's main sources of income. The metal workshop under Moholy-Nagy was another highly successful area, with a range of articles designed in nickel-silver or brass, often with black ebony handles. A style soon became evidence in the wide range of domestic wares – teapots, kettles, tea sets – a style based on the sphere, hemisphere and cylinder, within which apparently limiting formulæ designers such as Rittweger and Brandt produced pieces of extraordinary elegance, yet well suited to industrial production.

Despite these commercial successes, the history of the Bauhaus after 1928 was not a happy one. The Dessau Government was becoming strongly loaded with right-wing political groups: accusations of socialist leanings were hurled against the school, and more specifically at Gropius, at every discussion of the Bauhaus's budget, and in 1928 Gropius was driven to resign. He was succeeded by Hannes Meyer, who immediately set the Bauhaus on a new course of social responsibility. Eclectic tastes were dropped in favour of design for the masses, with the intention of producing inexpensive items, such as plywood furniture, that could be afforded by working people.

Under Meyer, the Bauhaus thrived economically, but growing political pressures forced his resignation after just two years. Mies van der Rohe, already an accomplished technician in steel and glass, took over. He introduced a greater emphasis on architectural theory, and concentrated once more on producing exclusive designs for a wealthy elite. Despite Mies' attempts to keep politics out of the Bauhaus, it was closed by the government in 1932 and the buildings were ransacked by the Nazis. A final attempt to revive the Bauhaus in a disused

Berlin factory came to an abrupt end when it was raided by police and on 10 August, 1933 Mies announced the final dissolution of the Bauhaus. It had existed a mere 14 years, but its influence was to be enduring. It was not so much the thrust of the early Bauhaus teaching, with its attempt to marry art and craft, that makes it so important in this context. More importantly, the school had provided a focus for the artistic, creative and intellectual life of post-World War I Germany, at times acting as a clearing house for many of the foremost artists and designers in Europe.

The influence of the Bauhaus was to continue to be felt abroad when, in the following years, Gropius, Mies van der Rohe, Moholy-Nagy (who had succeeded Itten in the metal workshop in 1923) and Breuer joined the exodus of artists and intellectuals from Nazi Germany to the United States. There, they achieved influential positions and disseminated the ideas of the Bauhaus, with Moholy-Nagy even going so far as to create a 'New Bauhaus' in Chicago in 1937. Mies van der Rohe became Dean of Architecture at the Illinois Institute of Technology, while Gropius took the Chair of Architecture at Harvard. Both were instrumental in ensuring the long-overdue acceptance of Modernism by the American establishment.

RIGHT *The Bauhaus weaving workshop produced carpets, woollen wall hangings and fabrics in strong shades, usually in geometric or abstract patterns. Their emphasis was often on texture, and they employed an extensive range of fabrics. Gunta Stölzl, one of their most influential figures, produced this slit gobelin with linen warp and cotton wool at the Dessau Bauhaus, 1927–8.*

Ludwig Mies van der Rohe, last director of the Bauhaus, was born the son of a German stone-cutter and was apprenticed to a furniture designer and architect, Peter Behrens. He started working for himself in 1912, and throughout the 1920s proved himself one of the foremost German architects in the functionalist 'steel and glass' style. His design submitted to the Berlin Friedrichstasse Skyscraper competition of 1921 epitomizes his vision: the building consisted of no more than an immense steel frame, sheathed in glass. Like the schemes of other Modernist architects, the design represented some sort of utopian solution, as if such purity was the necessary conclusion of functionalism.

In 1927 Mies was instrumental in bringing together the designs of modern architects for workers' housing in one project, the *Weissenhof Siedlung*. In an area of parkland overlooking the city of Stuttgart (today in West Germany) the work of Modernist architects such as Walter Gropius, Mart Stam, Le Corbusier, Peter Behrens and Mies himself was brought together to demonstrate modern solutions to the problem of creating cheap housing for workers. The buildings were characterized by the use of flat roofs and standardized parts, white-painted walls and rectilinear geometry, and as such did much to crystallize the new Modernist style, devoid of homage to what were seen as the ornamentation of previous decades. It is this utopian vision, expressed in many of the buildings of the *Siedlung*, which was the driving force behind what can loosely be called the Modern Movement.

In 1929 Mies was given the task of designing the German Pavilion for the Barcelona Exhibition. Created as a temporary showcase for German design, the pavilion was a brilliant exercise in construction, employing eight narrow steel supports to carry a thin slab which made up the roof. Like Rietveld's Schröder House, it comprised a series of planes at angles to each other, with the vertical panels of travertine and glass capped by the roof slab, and two pools to act as reflectors.

Like other designers of the time, Mies was concerned not only with the structure of his buildings but with the furnishings, and his

innovative chairs and tables – pioneering the use of nickel-plated tubing and black lacquered wood – were to be highly influential. Despite his role as director of the Bauhaus from 1930 to 33, his furniture designs disregard economy and concentrate on opulence. His two main chair designs – the Barcelona and the MR chairs – were to have tremendous impact on subsequent twentieth-century furniture. The MR was a cantilevered tubular steel chair designed in 1926 to 27 and the first version of the successful Weissenhof chair, designed for the Weissenhof housing development. The simple appearance is deceptive, more for aesthetic reasons than structural ones – his famous maxim was that 'God is in the details', and the chair was very carefully designed to give this air of simplicity. The Barcelona chair, designed for the German Pavilion in 1929, has been described as the single most brilliant piece of industrial furniture of the twentieth century. Like the MR, this forged steel-strip and leather chair, despite its apparent simplicity, is a design which requires complicated and careful production techniques.

LEFT *The Barcelona Chair by Mies van der Rohe.*

ABOVE *MR chairs by Mies van der Rohe.*

RIGHT Weissenhof Siedlung *houses, by Mart Stam, 1927. The crystallization of the Modern Movement came with the Stuttgart Exhibition of 1927 when, under the tutelage of Mies van der Rohe, Modernist architects were asked to build a 'settlement' in the new modern style. Mart Stam's design is characteristic of Modernist architecture with its flat roof, white walls and machine-made windows and railings.*

RIGHT *Pair of chairs by Robert Mallet-Stevens, 1927. The use of wood and fabric is a clever rethinking of the deckchair concept.*

BELOW RIGHT *Table lamp in brushed aluminium by Georges Le Chevallier, late 20s. Le Chevallier stressed the industrial, machine-made aspect of his fixtures by leaving screws clearly visible.*

BELOW *Fabric design by Hélène Henry, c1925. The self-taught Parisian's silk and rayon materials were noted for their thick, 'natural' look and their neutral blues.*

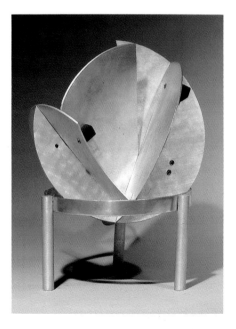

The principles and achievements of the Bauhaus school were a significant formative influence on certain French designers who reacted against the highly decorative aspects of Art Deco. The rallying point for French Modernism was the Union des Artistes Modernes, founded in 1930. Members included: René Herbst, Francis Jourdain, Hélène Henri, Robert Mallet-Stevens, Pierre Chareau, Raymond Templier, Edouard-Joseph Djo-Bourgeois, Eileen Gray, Le Corbusier, and Charlotte Perriand. These architects and designers rejected the excessive ornamentation characteristic of the Paris salons of the early 1920s, and gave priority to function over form. They designed furniture in materials such as steel, chrome and painted-metal tubes, in which individual elements were designed for mass production.

In their quest for *Le beau dans l'utile* ('beauty in the useful'), these French Modernists achieved genuine advances in style. For example, the chairs of Le Corbusier, notably his chaise longue of 1928, have become accepted as classics of design and are still in production. The changes that were in the air affected every aspect of domestic design. Modernist rugs by artists such as Jean Lurçat or Ivan da Silva Bruhns replaced the florid rugs and carpets associated with the Art Deco style; wall decorations were virtually eliminated. The designers and decorators working in this new style saw themselves as purists and as rationalists, although their brand of functionalism by no means precluded a sense of style. On the contrary, the best Modernist interiors were totally chic, though their icy perfection and often clinical appearance suggest that their designers have somehow overlooked their ultimate function as living spaces for imperfect humans. The welcome virtues of Modernist interiors were in their sense of space and their emphasis on light and cleanliness.

By the end of the 1920s, tubular-steel furniture was being created both by architects and furniture designers. The public was asked to reconsider the aesthetic merits of utilitarian, even humble materials such as steel and metal alloys for furniture production, in place of the proud and royal traditions of France's eighteenth-century cabinetmakers. Metal entered the home through the kitchen door – in the traditional manufacture of metal household utensils – after which it gradually worked its way into the other rooms of the house. Final and complete acceptance came in the selection of metal rather than wood for salon and dining-room furniture, to be seen and used by guests.

LEFT *Silver-plated cocktail shaker and six goblets designed by Desny, with Modernist streamlining.*

BELOW *Brooch of gold, onyx, enamel and diamonds by Gérard Sandoz, 1928, featuring strong geometric shapes.*

The architect-designer most responsible for formalizing international Modernism was Charles-Edouard Jeanneret, known as Le Corbusier (a pseudonym he adopted from 1920 onwards), whose *Vers une Architecture* (1923) proved to be one of the most significant publications of the twentieth century. In this series of essays Le Corbusier expounded a view of architecture at once severely functional and at the same time utopian. In 1921 he had stated his view that *'une maison est une machine à habiter'* ('a house is a machine for living in'), and in *Vers une Architecture* he went on to speak of houses 'built on the same principles as the Ford car'. He looked forward to the coming of the 'house-machine' – 'the mass-production house, healthy – ánd morally so too – and beautiful.'

His ideas were demonstrated at the Paris 1925 Exhibition, where his *L'Esprit Nouveau* pavilion was perhaps the most striking structure, and certainly the most controversial in terms of its then and future significance. The pavilion was merely a single apartment, taken like a drawer from a chest-of-drawers, from a large block of flats from his city of 3 million inhabitants of 1922. Rectangular, and cube-like, with large, plain windows, it was the very latest in Modernist architecture. The interior was stripped of what he considered abhorrent decorative art, with colour-washed walls and furnished with mass-produced standardized equipment such as cheap bentwood chairs. A model monoplane was hung on a wall like a trophy. The furnishings were rather boring and awkward, but the structure itself lived up to its title 'The New Spirit' – flooded with light and high ceilinged, its rooms and spaces practically designed.

A number of domestic commissions established Le Corbusier's reputation and climaxed with the Villa Savoye at Poissy (1928 to 1929), which neatly summarizes his self-proclaimed 'Five Points of a New Architecture' – a free plan, a free façade, *pilotis* (exposed and free-standing load-bearing piles, so that the house appears to stand on stilts), a terrace and ribbon windows. While appearing to implement his machine-inspired ideas, it also reveals a sculptural treatment of forms.

Le Corbusier designed a number of total plans for towns and cities, utopian in scale and intention; not surprisingly, these totalitarian schemes were never built. Not least of these projects was his plan for the *Ville Radieuse* ('Shining City'). Successful projects included the Maison de Refuge, Paris (1930 to 1933), a large building with a ship-like presence, one wall of which was almost entirely glass. The Swiss pavilion (1930 to 1931) which Le Corbusier designed for the Cité Universitaire, Paris, marks a shift in emphasis towards a more organic treatment of concrete. Like the Villa Savoye, the main body of the building is suspended above ground by means of supports. In place of the slender white *pilotis* are curved, robust bare-concrete pillars. The volumes within dictate the exterior, with the 'cells' of the student rooms expressed on the façade to form a grid.

Le Corbusier redefined furniture into three categories – chairs, tables and shelves – and designed standard pieces for the interiors of his buildings accordingly. Some of his innovative designs, such as the famous chaise longue, achieved both stylishness and practicality and are today regarded as icons of Modernism. On the whole, his chairs show the desire for 'anonymous' design that pervades the period – equipment, rather than art.

ABOVE *The Villa Savoye, Poissy, near Paris, by Le Corbusier, 1928–9. This villa displayed Le Corbusier's 'Five Points of a New Architecture' – a roof terrace,* pilotis, *a free-plan, strip windows, and a free composition of the façade.*

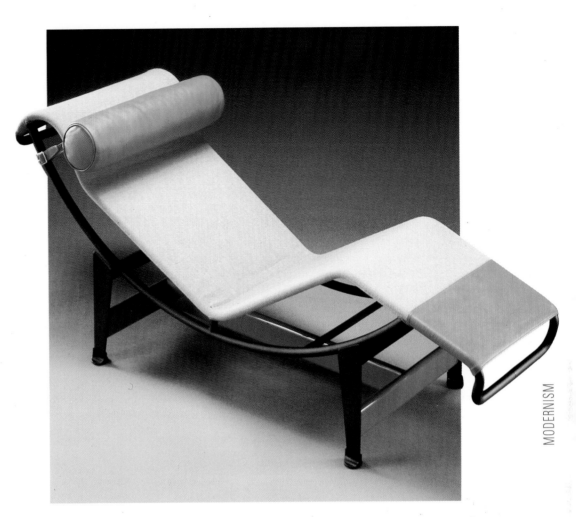

ABOVE *Le Corbusier's famous chaise longue of 1928.*

LEFT *Chair by Le Corbusier, 20s. Made from chromed-steel and upholstered in ponyskin, these chairs are typical of Le Corbusier's work in the quality and expense of the materials used.*

Modernism itself was in transition from its role as an architectural phenomenon born of sincere utopianism into that of an acceptably modern fashion. An exhibition held in New York in 1931–32, under the aegis of the Museum of Modern Art, was designed to bring the fact of the existence of Modernism to a wider audience. In the catalogue accompanying the exhibition, co-authors Henry-Russell Hitchcock and Philip Johnson coined the phrase 'The International Style'. According to Hitchcock and Johnson, buildings in the International Style were to follow precise aesthetic and construction principles – the conception of architectural space as volume and the technically perfect use of materials. The influence of Le Corbusier becomes important in that the International Style is characterized by attempts by the architects involved to induce the ideas of weightlessness in buildings by the use of cantilevered extensions. Through cantilevering, load-bearing elements of the building are shifted back into the interior, thus allowing for the construction of light spaces lit by what appear to be walls of glass.

Curiously enough, Hitchcock and Johnson railed against the skyscraper, which must be seen as the logical roof of Modernist building methods. First built in the nineteenth century, skyscrapers were at that time becoming more and more common, particularly in New York, with the construction of the Chrysler, General Electric and Empire State buildings, all dating from the 1930s in the post-International Style era. Johnson and Hitchcock identified that a building in the International Style should be constructed of steel, glass and reinforced concrete and should have a geometrically derived and organized appearance. Their mistrust of the skyscraper was derived from the ornamentation applied to buildings with rationalist construction at their heart.

Geometry, steel, glass and reinforced concrete are of course classic Modernist materials and their employment is a distinctively Modernist device, found as early as 1911 in

BELOW *De La Warr Pavilion, Bexhill-on-Sea, by Mendelsohn and Chermayeff, 1935–36. The use of cantilevering, concrete, standardized windows and rails can clearly be seen. This is a Modernist building in design and function.*

RIGHT *Empire State Building, New York, by Shreve, Lamb and Harmon, 1929–31. This is Skyscraper Style as opposed to International Style, but nonetheless modern in construction.*

Walter Gropius's Fagus Shoe Factory, in Alfeld.

There are obvious stylistic links between many buildings which employ Modernist construction techniques and yet are the result of either the injection of private capital, as in Le Corbusier's *Maisons Blanches* or the direction of status-seeking local councils with a sympathetic Modernist bent. For instance, Mendelsohn and Chermayeff built the De la Warr Pavilion in Bexhill, Sussex in 1935. It used the principles of cantilevering and the glass wall, and was obviously both a Modernist building and in the International Style. Likewise, Maxwell Fry's Sun House, built in Hampstead, London, in 1936, shared many of the qualities of Le Corbusier's Villa Stein (1926) at Garches, France, with its terraces, rectilinearity and skilful juggling of masses and voids, creating the lightness and modernity concomitant with the new modern architecture.

BELOW *Chaise longue in plywood, by Marcel Breuer for Isokon, 1935.*

Modernist icons such as Marcel Breuer's Wassily Chair owe their form not only to the vision of the designer, but to the properties of the materials from which they were made. The strength of tubular steel allowed for a lightweight design with flat leather surfaces intersecting to make an innovatory and comfortable armchair. The fact that Breuer named the chair after the Russian Constructivist painter, Wassily Kandinsky, hints at the interaction between those at the cutting edge of art and design at this time. Indeed, Constructivist art reveals its influence in the intersection of the flat leather surfaces of the Wassily Chair.

Plastics, too, made their impact at this time. These new synthetics found an interface with Modernism in their use by, amongst others, Serge Chermayeff and Wells Coates in Britain, notably in their designs for radio housings in the 1930s. Coates, like the Russian-born Chermayeff, was an architect, and the fact that architects were designing domestic objects designed for mass-production helped to introduce the ideas of modernity into the lives of

ordinary people. Technology was seen to enter the home on a grand scale, and what is more it came in a cabinet which expressed modernity in its look as well as its contents.

In the field of architecture, the use of reinforced concrete proved both practical and suited to the desired minimalist style. One product of the availability of new materials coupled with the quest for quality mass-production was the development of prefabricated buildings. In previous decades architecture for the masses had been derived from the cheapest possible application of traditional house-building techniques. Modernism sought to break away from this pattern and to answer the need for housing by employing mass-production techniques to the construction of housing. Therefore, for economic as well as aesthetic reasons, the walls, windows, drainage systems and some interior parts of Modernist architecture were prefabricated. An early example was Le Corbusier's Dom-ino housing scheme (1914 to 1915) to provide quickly erected, cheap dwellings. Designed as a kit, each unit consisted of a six-pillared reinforced concrete frame which supported cantilevered slabs of reinforced concrete. The walls no longer carried any weight so that they could be placed anywhere.

Both the birth and spread of Modernism were aided by the spread of extremist politics. The consolidation of the Communist regime, together with the growth of National Socialism in Germany during the late 1920s and 1930s, served to catalyze the spread of Modernism. Kandinsky, El Lissitzky and Chermayeff all left Russia for Germany. From there, Chermayeff, together with Gropius, Eric Mendelsohn, Breuer and later Mies van der Rohe, made the trip to England and then to the United States.

However, this migration did not occur largely until after Hitler had obtained power in 1933. Up to this time, Modernism was employed in the construction of housing for ordinary people – but never on the kind of utopian scale which its progenitors had hoped for. There were, however, some examples of the successful use of rationalist principles in the construction of housing, such as Gropius's Siemensstadt development in Berlin (1929 to 1930), and these estates became places of pilgrimage for those who wished to see the precepts of Modernism put into practice.

BELOW *Tea service by Margaret Heymann-Löbenstein, 1930. Löbenstein trained at the Bauhaus from 1919 to 1922, and her design conforms to the early Bauhaus ideal of combining the Modernist 'machine' aesthetic with the marks of craft production techniques.*

BELOW *Ekco Model AD36 wireless by Wells Coates, 1935.*

MODERNISM

Modernism was to have a profound influence in the field of industrial design in the late 1920s and 1930s. The Industrial Revolution had long since taken place, the Machine Age was flourishing, and the design of handsome domestic objects, large and small, static and kinetic, was an inevitable outcome. Everything from cigarette lighters, cameras, toasters and vacuum cleaners to furniture, cars, trains and aeroplanes drew the attention of designers, who 'restyled' fairly new appliances such as electric lamps, fans, fires, refrigerators and radios, and 'revolutionized' objects that had been in use for centuries, such as clocks, teapots and scales.

If there is one thing which characterizes the new designs of the consumer durables of the interwar years, particularly in the United States, it is the encasement of the working parts in a smoothly modern housing. The vocabulary of the industrial designer was primarily that of industry, and the byword was 'streamlining' – that is, smoothing away the bumps and angles to produce a bullet – or teardrop-shape, which offered the least resistance in terms of physics. The materials used were metal, wood, glass, plastic and other new or improved ingredients, and the final products were glossy, chic and extremely *moderne*, in line with the broadly held functionalist theories used to legitimate the work of the industrial designers. Ease of manufacture was a strongly determinant factor in the way things began to look by the 1930s, yet streamlining became a phenomenon which transcended the purely functional and, like Art Deco, it became a name for yet another form of applied decoration. The streamform had become a symbolic expression of a new age of efficiency and speed – an age in which the forward thrust of intellectual thought expressed in art and architecture was borne faster forward by hunger for the modernity of a newly designed world.

The 1930s saw the advent of the age of consumerism, with portable objects among the first to be 'transformed' by industrial designers: irons, staplers, pencil-sharpeners, tape dispensers, tabletop and desk lamps, kitchen and factory tools, drinking glasses and vases were all produced along the lines of the new industrial-

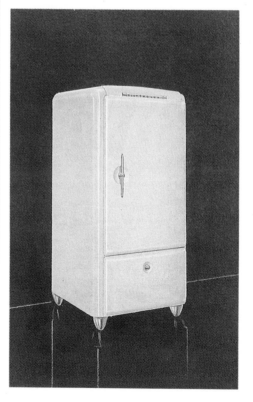

RIGHT *The Chrysler 'Airflow' car incorporated streamform styling of a quasi-scientific origin. When it was introduced in 1934, it was too far beyond contemporary experience of what a car should look like for the public to accept this modern shape. Nevertheless, by the time it was withdrawn in 1938, the streamform was often seen in the exterior styling of the American car.*

LEFT *Plastic salt and pepper shakers, souvenirs of 1939 New York's World Fair and featuring the Fair emblem of the Trylon and Perisphere, and its official colours of blue and orange.*

LEFT *Electrolux refrigerator designed by Raymond Loewy in the late 30s. It echoed the basic concept of his revolutionary Goldspot model for Sears Roebuck in 1935, with the whole encased in a sleek, white-enamelled box on low legs – but its angles and hardware were less prominent and geometric.*

Chrysler 'Airflow', 1935.

ABOVE *Enamelled-metal*
electric iron, designed
by Christian Barman
for HMV in 1934. The
integration of handle
with body results in a
streamlined yet
somewhat inchoate
shape.

design creed. The now-familiar pistol-shaped hairdrier made its first appearance in the 1920s. Household appliances such as vacuum cleaners and washing machines were reassessed not merely as functional objects but as suitable subjects for the aesthetic considerations of designers. Naturally, streamlining principles were applied to objects that moved – automobiles, aeroplanes, boats, trailers, and, perhaps most successfully trains.

Some streamlined objects have remained in production for many years, or are experiencing a comeback of sorts. On the whole, though, the era was short-lived but exciting, and its glorious postscript (some say apotheosis) was the 1939 World's Fair in New York, which highlighted the 'World of Tomorrow'. Its symbol, the simple but dramatic trylon and perisphere, represented limitless flight and controlled stasis. The exhibition's futuristic displays and pavilions in effect marked the end of the beginning of Modernism, a period which had opened with the 1925 Exposition in Paris.

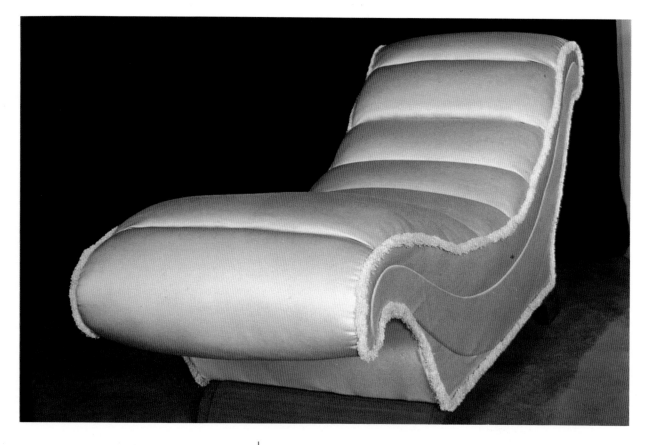

In Britain, Modernism was adopted largely in the field of interior design, whether in the very English intellectuality of Grant and Bell or Francis Bacon's 'constructivist room', with white walls, circular glass tables and mirrors and neutral coloured rugs woven in 'thought patterns'. In 1927 Syrie Maugham uncovered her 'all-white room' in her seventeenth-century Chelsea house. Some said she had originated the all-white idiom, others claimed it was Arundell Clarke or Da Silva Bruhns; whatever the truth, the scheme was widely adopted, as in Claridges all-white restaurant.

The turning-point for interior design had come with the 1925 Paris Exhibition. Germany, and therefore the Bauhaus, had been excluded from exhibiting and it was not until 1930–1 that the Salon des Artistes-Décorateurs included a Bauhaus section.

The 1925 Exhibition was dominated by the work of Ruhlmann, Süe et Mare and Lalique, but England's reaction was summed up by the *Architectural Review* of that year: 'Unquestionably every Englishman who visits the pavilions and stands of the modern French *ensembliers*

will ask himself whether he would care to live among such impeccable surroundings from which cosiness is markedly absent . . . But little doubt that our Englishman, mindful of fireside joys, of capacious easy chairs, will, perhaps, admire, then turn aside and leave such artificialities to the exhibition and to France.'

The exhibition did influence one important aspect of British design, the Modernist rug. The American poster designer Edward McKnight Kauffer, encouraged by Marion Dorn, first used Cubist abstract designs in rugs and from 1928 their work was hand-woven at the Wilton Royal Carpet Factory, which also commissioned Marian Pepler, John Tandy and Ronald Grierson.

Gradually the new ideas did begin to find expression in England. The real discipline of the Bauhaus furniture, founded upon geometry, was scarce, but modern design, square furniture or the later rounded curves in plain veneer, were to be found at Curtis Moffat's Fitzroy Square galleries, at Betty Joel Ltd. at 25 Knightsbridge, at Heal's.

Betty Joel is best-known for her simple, unpretentious pieces of furniture designed for the smaller house and her clever use of unusual woods such as laurel, greywood, sycamore, Queensland walnut and bird's eye maple. She founded Betty Joel Ltd in 1919 and successfully exhibited at the Exhibition of British Industrial Art in 1933, supplying the Russell Workshops with their designs from 1934 before retiring in 1937.
ABOVE *Chaise longue, beechwood upholstered in cream silk, c1930.*

Eileen Gray was born in Ireland in 1879, trained at the Slade School of Art in London and then became an apprentice at a lacquer workshop. She worked all over Europe during the next 30 years with many of the great names of the twentieth century, and her far-seeing furniture, object and building designs were distinctive *moderne* exercises. Some of her early works are opulent, extravagant, even whimsical confections, but most of her later designs are practical and elegant modern classics.

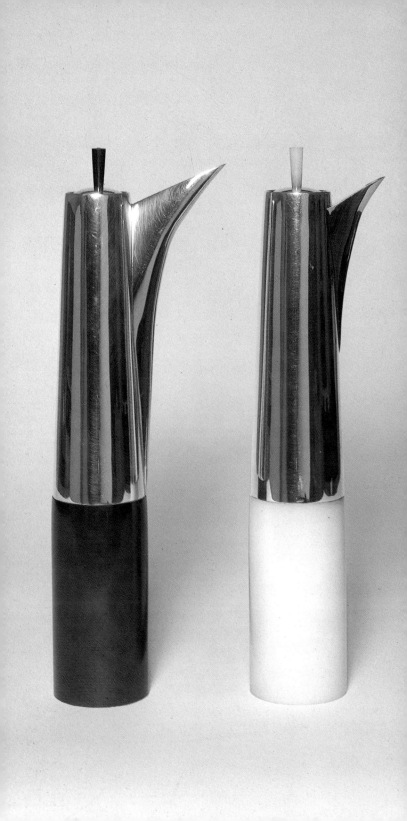

5. POST *war*

developments (1940–1990)

THE EARLY 40s WERE STAGNANT YEARS IN THE CREATIVE ARTS: THE WAR EFFORT CLAIMING SO MUCH ENERGY, SO MANY RESOURCES. Indeed, even the late 40s remained austere years in a world rebuilding and reassessing itself after the destruction of the war. Christian Dior may have launched his extravagant New Look in 1947, but in Britain rationing remained a way of life until the 50s. From the ruins of the war years, however, there emerged a new sense of hope, an optimism which was to survive through the late 50s and 60s before coming to grief in the essentially cynical 70s.

Industry set about rebuilding itself in the immediate postwar period, exploring new technologies and materials, among them the new synthetics and alloys which were often the direct product of wartime experiment. After the prewar era of technological dreams and nightmares, in which the machine had become a love-hate symbol in the arts, the technological age had at last arrived. Germany and Japan, their industries destroyed by defeat, were forced to rebuild from the drawing board and have risen from the ashes as the most industrially advanced countries, setting the pace during the 60s and 70s.

The 50s and 60s were decades of new affluence and technology was welcomed into middle- and working- class homes in terms of consumer hardware which raised standards of living as never before.

The lead in this new consumerism came from the United States, where the brash and confident styling and packaging of consumer goods, the exaggerated scale of supermarkets and cars, freeways and skyscrapers made 'The Big Country' into the very image of the promised land. Perhaps the most striking feature of the American import was its emphasis on a previously ignored market, the young, who for the first time had money to spend and a determination to carve out a style for themselves.

The following decades would see no more

BELOW The age of mass media: by the 50s no home was complete without a television. In the United States alone the number of people owning sets rose by 47 million over the decade.

LEFT *The most important event to affect the design of mass-produced goods in postwar Britain was the Festival of Britain in 1951. For a time the 'Fesival Style' could be seen everywhere. For a ration-weary public, the Festival represented everything that utility goods and austerity were not. The effect of the exhibition on British design and 'Contemporary Style' in the immediate years was far-reaching, but in the end short-lived. As the writer Michael Frayn pointed out, 'the fashions it set in architecture and design were quickly copied, became clichés, and eventually looked vulgar against the growing affluence of the 50s.'*

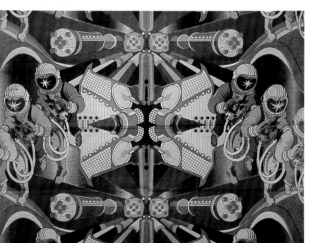

LEFT *The Space Age brought not only new technology, with such innovations as the nonstick frying pan (a spin-off from NASA's spacecraft technology), but a vivid source of imagery. Rocket ships and spacemen entered the lexicography of the decorative arts, as in 'Spacewalk', designed by Sue Thatcher in 1969.*

'total' movements in the arts like Art Nouveau or Art Deco, but a plethora of energizing new influences. The Space Age was to begin in 1957, with the launch of the first Russian Sputnik. A science-fiction idea became a reality, which in turn has provided a rich fund of stylish imagery and has nourished what is still essentially a fantasy. The decade of the conquest of space, the 'Swinging Sixties', saw the triumph of youth culture with a frenetic explosion of talent in the arts: young, raw talents breaking down class and age barriers, creating a new aristocracy revolving around the worlds of fashion, advertising, film-making, commercial photography, Pop music and Pop Art, which continues to be a pervasive influence in the decorative arts.

The postwar years were also to lead into the High Technology age. Unprecedented technological advances over the last 30 years have produced new materials – plastics, acrylics, fibreglass, stainless steel – and techniques, with dramatic social changes following in their wake. The late 1970s saw the beginning of a new era of mass communications, with a flood of satellite televisions, photocopiers, facsimile machines, desk-top computers and international dialling codes. The spread of consumerism amongst a newly affluent middle class led to increasingly widespread awareness of style in domestic and product design, and mass production finally asserted its supremacy over the individually hand-wrought. The traditional barriers between different art disciplines began to crumble.

The postwar years have seen a host of new directions within the arts, amongst them Pop Art and the drug culture-inspired psychedelic movement of the sixties, in the work of British and West Coast American artists. There have been Craft Revivals and, antithetically, a move towards a High-Tech industrial style. We have seen International Modernism, Organic Modernism and neo-Modernism. Post-Modernism emerged in the 1970s as a reaction against the severe cubic shapes and abstract geometry of Modernism, while more recently Deconstructivism harks back to the Russian Constructivists of the 1920s and 1930s.

In purely stylistic terms the contemporary era unfolds in a pattern of more or less identifiable phases, though the overlap, the sometimes contradictory parallel developments and the unbroken thread of some influences would render inaccurate any very rigid analysis. The decorative arts owe a considerable debt to the fine arts and to prewar stylistic and ethical precursors, notably in the continuing evolution of the international Modernist aesthetic.

The first pointers towards a distinctive new style in design and decoration came in the early 40s from the United States where Charles Eames and Eero Saarinen were evolving the language of Organic Modernism, exploring free forms and the balance of slender lines and abstract masses which were to become so distinctive a feature of the postwar years. In the hands of essentially rational rather than decorative designers Organic Modernism became a style which somehow seemed to reconcile the conflicts between form and func-

tion explored since the Art Nouveau era. The clean-lined logic of international Modernism combined with the effortless grace of curvilinear Art Nouveau, with more than a nod at the American Streamlined Moderne of the 30s. In architecture the style was to find a late but perfect expression in Frank Lloyd Wright's Guggenheim Museum, completed in 1959, and in the taut, elegant, free-flowing curves of Saarinen's T.W.A. Terminal at Kennedy Airport of 1961.

The free form acquired a symbolic decorative value and was to be found in every medium. Its painterly origins were in the symbolic abstract forms of the Surrealist painters. Charles Eames' prototype *chaise* of 1948 is a pure exercise in the new style. Raised on the distinctive thin legs, which he had been the first to introduce, the amoeboid, free-form seat, asymmetrical, curving in every direction and with an off-centre cut-out, might have been the creation of a sculptor.

LEFT *The High-Tech Industrial Style of interior decoration which emerged in 1978 was a response to the contemporary fascination with a technological ideal of functional environment which adopted industrially manufactured objects for domestic use. The interior of the Industrial Style London shop 'Joseph' incorporates new and classic Industrial Style elements designed in 1979.*

LEFT *Plastic Tulip Chair by Eero Saarinen. Though born in Finland in 1916, where his father was a major architect, he grew up in Chicago where he worked closely with Charles Eames. The fruits of their partnership formed at the Cranbrook Academy of Art, Michigan, US are easy to see in his soft-outlined, sculptural seats. Saarinen said of his pedestal design, which has become one of the lasting images of the 1960s, 'the underside of typical chars and tables makes a confusing and restless world . . . I wanted to clear up the slum of legs.'*

LEFT *Solomon R. Guggenheim Museum, New York, by Frank Lloyd Wright, 1943–59. More like a multistorey car park than a museum from its outward appearance, the Guggenheim's characteristic form has become a visual icon in its own right.*

THE FIFTIES

The 1950s were a time of change after the postwar Depression. New synthetic materials and a range of new products were being produced to satisfy the demands of the newly affluent consumer society. Cars, televisions and refrigerators became essential status symbols. Youth came into its own in the 1950s with the recognition of a specifically teenage market, rock-'n'-roll took the world by storm, and in the middle 50s a counterculture of 'Angry Young Men' and the 'Beat Generation' emerged.

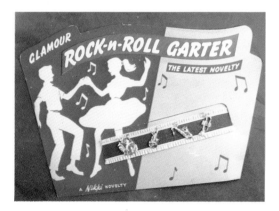

ABOVE *As the rock 'n' roll culture became more pervasive, manufacturers cashing in on its popularity came up with more and more ideas for novelties.*

ABOVE *The most popular interior design look of the 1950s was smooth and streamlined, with built-in coordinating kitchens becoming the ideal. The kitchen was also made more of a comfortable family room. In fact, distinctions between the 'correct' use of different rooms began to blur, and designers began to move towards more open-plan interiors, with 'areas' rather than rooms.*

RIGHT *Silver-plated coffee service by Sabattini showing the influence of Expressionism in the 1950s.*

LEFT *'Chickenwire'chair designed by Harry Bertoia for Hans and Florence Knoll, which he envisaged as 'mostly made of air, just like sculpture.' The thin, tubular steel legs were characteristic of 50's furniture design.*

ABOVE *Italian shoes with the newly-fashionable stiletto heels that aroused strong criticism in the 50s.*

LEFT *The fashionable fabrics of the early 50s owed their inspiration to trends in abstract art, as in this printed rayon designed by the British artist Marion Mahler for David Whitehead Ltd.*

The fashionable abstract free form was very often counterbalanced by thin lines, which found a specific and highly popular area of exploitation in the 'molecular-structure' motifs which so perfectly expressed the optimistic postwar mood of scientific progress. Explored in depth by the Festival Pattern Group in a project which began in May 1949, molecular structures became the basis for patterns in every medium and indeed for certain elements of the very structure of the Festival of Britain.

The thin, scratchy line, however, developed a quite independent life of its own and was used in graphic and three-dimensional contexts, often in romantic and whimsical frivolities, such as the cartoons and creations of the British Rowland Emmett, or the sweet lovers of French illustrator Peynet, in a magical and sentimental postwar Paris.

In furniture design two important examples of the thin line are Ernest Race's 'Antelope' chair, designed for the Festival of Britain, and the American, Harry Bertoia's 'chickenwire' chairs. The random graffiti of the American Abstract Expressionists were soon absorbed into the language of the decorative arts. Jackson Pollock's giant canvases formed appropriately modish backdrops to fashion photographs by Cecil Beaton. Pollock, one of the great stylists of American art, provided an inspiration to pattern-makers, as did the lesser names of the new Abstract schools.

BELOW *The typical thin scratchy lines and counter-balancing masses of the postwar years on a British fabric.*

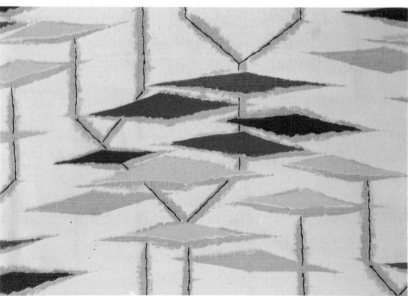

LEFT *The popular 'trattoria' style is well demonstrated in this Franco and Mario restaurant interior. The vaulted ceiling and tiled floor are characteristic features.*

RIGHT *French painted wood and metal coat stand of the 1950s.*

The postwar mood of optimism, which explored with such enthusiasm the language of Organic Modernism and which delighted in the magical elements of Surrealism and the decorative whimsy of the 'Festival (of Britain) Style', found perhaps its most symbolic expression in the building of the new Coventry Cathedral, completed in 1962. Basil Spence's design involved the collaboration of Britain's leading artists and craftsmen and forms a setting for such *tours de force* as Sutherland's magnificent tapestry and John Piper's magical stained-glass windows and less well-known details such as Elizabeth Frink's lectern or Hans Coper's monumental ceramic candle-holders.

The romantic flush of postwar optimism in decoration and design mellowed into the essential seriousness, the concern with good taste which characterized the more restrained elegance of 'Fifties Contemporary' and which marked the resurgence of International Modernism. Enter Scandinavian design on to the international market. Re-enter Mies van der Rohe, Bauhaus father of international Modernism, with American architect Philip Johnson holding his coat tails. Mies and his disciples, now based in the United States, were summoned from the wings to build the monuments of postwar prosperity. The towering black steel and plate glass rectangular blocks of Mies's Lake Shore Drive, Chicago, apartment buildings set the pattern in 1950. The Seagram Building, New York, which he designed in 1958 in partnership with Philip Johnson, is a monument to the continuing influence of International Modernism, as are the countless corporate blocks which tower over the skylines of almost every major international city. In 1955, Knoll International started the manufacture and distribution of Mies's classic prewar furniture designs.

As International Modernism, an architectural theorists and a domestic style for the design-conscious, reasserted itself, there developed an irrepressible counter-movement, the voice of popular culture which found its brashest, crudest, yet most stylish expression in the postwar architectural phenomenon of the twentieth-century's city of light, Las Vegas. Architect Robert Venturi, a key spokesman and exponent of 'Post-Modernism' has expressed the dilemma in his *Learning from Las Vegas*: 'Modern architecture has not so much excluded the commercial vernacular as it has tried to take it over by inventing and enforcing a vernacular of its own, improved and universal. It has rejected the combination of fine art and crude art.

The potency of Las Vegas as a symbol of popular culture has been perfectly expressed by Tom Wolfe who describes the city as '. . . the Versailles of America.' 'The important thing', he wrote, 'about the building of Las Vegas is not that the builders were gangsters but that they were proles. They celebrated, very early, the new style of life of America – using the money pumped in by the war to show a prole vision . . . of style.' And what style!

RIGHT *Seagram Building, New York, by Mies van der Rohe with Philip Johnson, 1954–8. Mies van der Rohe's scheme for a glass office block in 1921 was prophetic: at the time it was structurally inconceivable, but within 35 years the idea had become a practicality.*

LEFT *The sparkling lights of Las Vegas, the city described by Tom Wolfe as 'the Versailles of America.'*

'That fantastic skyline! Las Vegas' neon sculpture, its fantastic 15-storey-high display signs, parabolas, boomerangs, rhomboids, trapezoids, and all the rest of it are already the staple diet of the American landscape. They soar in shapes before which the existing language of art history is helpless. I can only attempt to supply names – Boomerang Modern, Flash Gordon Ming-Alert Spiral . . . Mint Casino Elliptical, Miami Beach Kidney . . . Palette Curvilinear.'

The emergence in the States of a truly popular art, a cult of style which was essentially vulgar and, as such, has remained largely anonymous, ignored by 'serious' design history, found its expression in the seeming litter of the urban landscape, in the signs and neon games, distilled to the point of self-caricature in Las Vegas, and in the exaggerated styling of motor cars.

It was this language of disposable, consumer reality which was to fund the image bank of Pop Art, a movement which found its earliest partisans in England, in the Independent Group of the Institute of Contenporary Arts. The crystallization of the 'Pop' ethic came in 1956 with the Whitechapel Art Gallery exhibition 'This is Tomorrow', which introduced many

RIGHT *The American Dream is epitomized to the point of caricature in the exaggerated styling of ultra-streamlined cars.*

LEFT *Psychedelic imagery inspired a highly fertile era in graphic art, most notably in the by-products of the music industry such as this record sleeve for Cream's album 'Disraeli Gears', 1967, by illustrator Martin Sharp and photographer Bob Whittaker.*

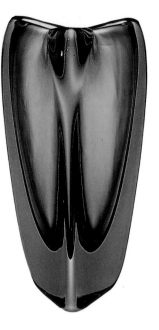

Throughout the 1960s Scandinavian glass design was the benchmark of 'good taste.' Its keynote was simplicity and practicality combined with good design, and its cool clean lines and common-sense detailing appealed to the postwar generation.

of the key themes of Pop Art: Marilyn Monroe, giant beer bottles, advertising ephemera and presented what is often cited as the first Pop picture, Richard Hamilton's collage *Just What is it That Makes Today's Homes so Different, so Appealing?* In this, a caricature consumer couple, a Charles Atlas-like figure and a sequin-trimmed pin-up, are set awkwardly in a photomontage home surrounded by consumer hardware – on the lampshade a giant shield from the Ford motor company, on the wall a comic-strip frame from *True Romance*. It was too early for them to have a 'genuine' Lichtenstein.

Pop, which had drawn on popular consumer imagery, in turn inspired a 'Pop' style in the applied arts, a fad in interior, graphic and fashion design which reached a peak in the late 60s and early 70s. The most enduring legacy, however, of Pop Art and of the concurrent Hard-Edged Abstractionist schools of painting of the 60s has been a dramatic new attitude to colour. The decade of Frank Stella, Elsworth Kelly, Morris Louis and Kenneth Noland saw the advent of sharp primary colours within the applied arts. These painters found the ideal colours, hard and synthetic for the synthetic materials in which so many objects were now manufactured.

THE SIXTIES

The 'Swinging Sixties' saw the recognition and establishment of a distinct youth culture: not only did young people account for a larger proportion of the population than ever before, they also had more leisure time and – importantly – more money. Under youth patronage fashion and music blossomed: the sound of the Beatles could be heard down every corridor and the miniskirt shocked parents the world over.

RIGHT *Living furniture by Terence Conran, made in the 60s. Conran opened his first Habitat shop in 1964, with the avowed intention of bringing good taste to a mass market, and hit a commercial goldmine with an amalgam of mainstream Modernist and reassuringly cosy 'good taste' styles.*

RIGHT *Designers continued to explore new forms. This fibreglass desk chair by Jean Lele, c1969, exploits the strength and ease of construction of the material to create an integral sculptural environment for the user.*

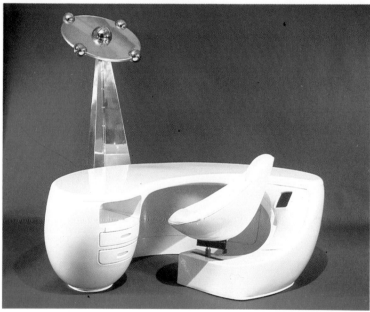

OPPOSITE, RIGHT *The pop-music industry – under the patronage of a young generation with a new spending power – elevated its moneymakers to the status of film stars, and a huge industry catered for pop idols' fans. No other group during the 60s could match the Beatles' success. The polka dot cotton dress with portrait heads of all four Beatles and a guitar was designed for usherettes at a Beatles' concert.*

RIGHT *One of the themes of youth culture of the early 60s was the future seen as some kind of science-fiction adventure. Space-age clothing, pioneered by Courrèges, materialized from Paris. This 'Cosmos' dress from Balmain in 1967 exhibited the trend toward simple geometric shapes and shorter hemlines.*

RIGHT *The influence of Surrealism: bracelet watch by Salvador Dali, 1960.*

The 60s was a richly diverse decade of stylistic trends. Pop and Hard Edge were dominant influences. Op and Kinetic Art made a short-lived but effective mark. Op Art, notably for a brief season around 1965, enjoyed a considerable influence in every aspect of design, from fashion and interior design to graphics and even film, where it soon lent itself to parody by William Klein in the joke Op Art scenes in his film *Qui Etes-vous Polly Magoo?* of 1967. Bridget Riley's or Victor Vasarely's patterns were never really intended to be worn or lived in.

A notable feature of the sixties was the revival of Art Nouveau, a revival first inspired by the Museum of Modern Art's major 1960 survey exhibition, 'Art Nouveau – Art and Design at the Turn of the Century.' This was followed in 1963 by a major retrospective of the work of the highly decorative graphic artist Alphonse Mucha at the Victoria and Albert Museum.

Side-by-side, incongruously, with this cult of the decadent age of Art Nouveau came the cult of the images of today, the symbols of speed and the Space Age. *Vogue* and other magazines illustrated futuristic silver rooms filled with metal furniture and gadgetry, and such fashions as the 'silver paper suit, the ultimate space-age adventure . . .' photographed by David Bailey in British *Vogue* of January 1967. No designer caught this mood more effectively than Paris couturier André Courrèges with his 'Clothes of the Future' which made so forceful an impact in 1965.

Perhaps the most fascinating spontaneous outburst of style of the decade, however, came in the 60s with the cult, the ideology, but above all the rich imagery of the so-called 'flower children.' The movement took shape in 1967 and combined an endearing *faux-naïf* romanticism with the more sinister exploration of the hallucinatory state, providing the exotic imagery of psychedelic experience. Psychedelic imagery, combined with borrowings from Art Nouveau and with a new palette – the vibrant, acid colours of the so-called acid trip – provided the basis of a highly fertile era in graphic art, most notably in the by-products of the music industry, posters and record sleeves.

ABOVE *Memorial window by Tim Lewis in All Saints Church, Oystermouth, Wales, 1977.*

A major ingredient of the 'hippie' cult was the fashion for ethnic clothing and interior decoration, the by-product of a naive, if deeply-felt ideological rejection of materialism. The look was perfectly captured by Talitha Getty, wife of the late Paul Getty's son Eugène. Although, ironically, this was in itself a new materialism. Mrs Getty was photographed, seated cross-legged in 'rich gypsy' clothes in her Rome drawing room in which '. . . the atmosphere is even more like that of an Eastern Bazaar: North African antiques are scattered about the room, a shrine to Buddha stands against one wall. The lighting is diffuse . . . scented joss sticks burn.'

LEFT *Mother's House, Philadelphia, by Robert Venturi, 1962–4. This was one of the first buildings to make the bold move away from the cubes and right angles of most Modernist architecture.*

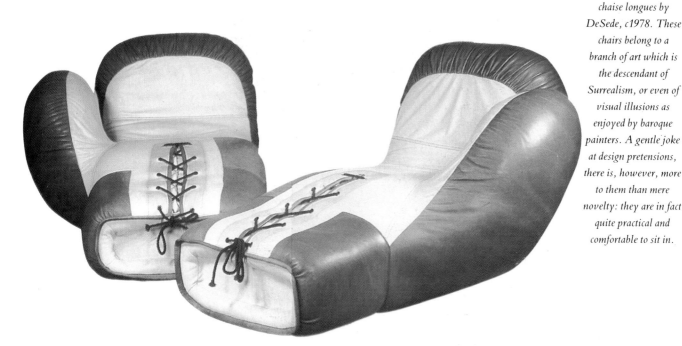

LEFT *Boxing Glove chaise longues by DeSede, c1978. These chairs belong to a branch of art which is the descendant of Surrealism, or even of visual illusions as enjoyed by baroque painters. A gentle joke at design pretensions, there is, however, more to them than mere novelty: they are in fact quite practical and comfortable to sit in.*

The young generation eventually and inevitably awoke from this dream and the transition into the 70s was an unsentimental one. The visual arts could not escape the realities of our environment and the 'hippie' cult was seen for what it was, a defiant but futile expression of escapist romanticism.

In painting, the turn of the decade was marked by a strong return to realism with a group of American painters evolving a style variously described as 'Photo-', 'Hyper', 'New' or 'Sharp-Focus' Realism, a style which met with the almost universal disapprobation of those art critics and commentators who had made so much wordage of the more painterly Pop, but above all of the various postwar abstract movements.

New Realism, however, met with a considerable popularity for it expressed a glossy, lovingly polished interpretation of the imagery of the urban environment. Perhaps the 'serious' critics resented the photographic nature of this realism and the painters' ability to bestow an undeniable beauty on the colours, materials

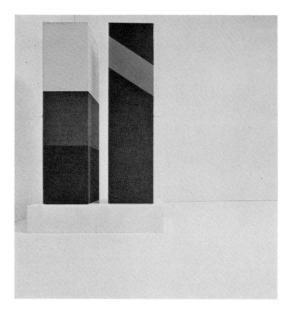

LEFT *Prototype models of wardrobes by Eileen Sottsass, 1966. A remarkable application of Fine Art styles to furniture design by this brilliant Italian.*

RIGHT *French plastic bracelet, c1970.*

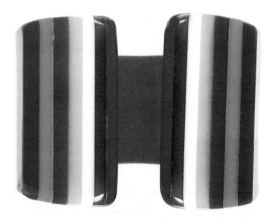

ABOVE *Design for shelving and clothing rails for the Mr Freedom shop by Jon Weallans, c1970.*

and textures of parking lot or store-front, neon-sign or motor vehicle. The style, beloved of art directors, transformed the American urban landscape into an aesthetic treat, exaggerating the beauty of polished chrome, plate-glass reflections and neon strips. The vibrant colour of Astroturf seemed more appealing than its natural alternative.

It is more difficult to characterize the 70s than the preceding decades, without the advantages of an extended hindsight, yet certain moods, certain elements already stand out. There is no doubt, for instance, that the New Realists heralded a very positive new aesthetic – frank, hard, cynical, arguably making a virtue of necessity, in fact accepting and enjoying the potential beauty of today's environment and today's materials, seeing the beauty in the man-made, the vulgar, even disposable,

enjoying the artifice of the saturated colours, the dynamic primaries which had first appeared in the decorative arts in the late 60s.

The cold polish of chromium-plated steel was enjoyed for its hard chic, without any of the bright-eyed idealism of previous generations. The symbols of the future became available realities in the decade of supersonic travel. The conveyor tubes of Paris' Charles de Gaulle airport were designed for use, not as the space-age set of a futuristic film. The architectural monument to this new frankness is, of course, the Paris Centre Pompidou designed by the Anglo-Italian team of Richard Rogers and Renzo Piano. Its sibling, on a reduced scale, is the British Sainsbury Centre for the Visual Arts, Norwich, designed by Norman Foster and opened in 1978.

The emergence of Post-Modernism as a

mode of thought in architecture found perhaps its most iconoclastic expression in the series of Best Products showrooms built across the United States to the designs of the Site Inc. team led by James Wines. Peeling, crumbling walls with piles of fallen bricks and a raw-edged notch in the brick structure to replace the standard entranceway became features of these humorous, controversial but much acclaimed projects started in 1972.

In domestic design and decoration the appreciation of the intrinsic beauty in the tough serviceability of industrially conceived hardware became a fashion and found a name in the 'High-Tech' style of the late 70s.

The other side of the coin, the sinister underside to the chic surface of the super-cool 70s was the spiritual emptiness which expressed itself in various brands of nihilistic behaviour, from political terrorism to the savage visual imagery and music of Punk. Andy Warhol expressed this mood in his usual ironical way. 'I believe that everyone should live in one big empty space. It can be a small space as long as it's clean and empty. I like the Japanese way of rolling everything up and locking it away in cupboards. But I wouldn't even have the cupboards because that's hypocritical.'

The potency and appetite of the commercial machine, however, came to dominate every aspect of life and transform even nihilistic concepts into marketable commodities. The Punk movement found its true graphic expression in such short-lived minority publications as *Anarchy in the U.K.*, but anarchy must constantly change its spots if it is to survive the inexorable machine of commerce. The apparel of anarchy becomes teenage fashion. Symbol becomes product.

BELOW *The Lexicon 83 DL6 typewriter designed for Olivetti by a team led by Mario Bellini, 1976. The design was amongst 25 selected in 1977 by* Fortune *magazine as the best examples of industrial design on the US market.*

ABOVE *An increasingly important element on contemporary design has been frank exposure of mechanisms, after a period of elaborate cosmetic concealment, as in this late 70s British clock.*

RIGHT *The 'Sovereign' pocket calculator designed for the British firm Sinclair Radionics Ltd. by a team led by John Pemberton. The soft-contoured casing of satin finish stainless steel, rationalized key system and red display-panel combine to make this a classic of modern industrial design.*

The commercial realities of the 70s remained a factor in design in the 80s. However, one design field which was to make a comeback was architecture, which had suffered from the economic recession of the 70s when many large building projects suffered and some indeed were abandoned. The 80s saw a resurgence. In fact, by the middle of the decade architecture was conspicuously fashionable. Smart clothes and 'designer' goods shops from New York to Paris and London to Tokyo proudly displayed copies of the more stylish architectural magazines, and such celebrated buildings as Richard Rogers' Paris Pompidou Centre featured on record sleeves. Shops also sprang up to deal with the new vogue for architect-designed consumer goods, and some architects found themselves better known for their kettle design than for their latest building. New York's Museum of Modern Art and London's Royal Academy ran major architectural exhibitions, and even the heir to the throne of England got in on the act – causing controversy with his criticism of modern architectural designs – 'monstrous carbuncles' – and attracting the wrath of the

ABOVE *Canary Wharf, London, 1988. London Docklands – Europe's largest building site.*

RIGHT *Louvre extension, Paris, 1988. Ieoh Ming Pei's transparent glass pyramid makes no attempt to blend with the surrounding buildings but rather complements them.*

profession for what many felt to be his rather reactionary taste.

In many ways the International Style and Modern Movements had brought the torrent of criticism down upon themselves with their puritanical, Bauhaus-influenced approach to architecture, in which function was all-important. The buildings which resulted from this philosophy were intended to change people for the better, but only succeeded in alienating their inhabitants and discrediting the movements and modern architecture in general. Indeed, instead of improving the lot of the working class, the Modern Movement's low-cost housing actually worsened it. Social problems grew too great to be ignored; conformity began to be replaced by individualism.

The 80s saw a series of spectacular architectural projects in France, initiated by the President François Mitterrand, which would leave a physical reminder of his administration for posterity. In Britain, London's Docklands became the largest building site in Europe, and in the United States various imaginative schemes were launched to regenerate inner city areas and city centres. Various new patrons also appeared on the scene, anxious to encourage the new talent and vibrancy.

While private or individual patronage had all but disappeared (apart from a few brave entrepreneurs such as Peter Palumbo in Britain), companies such as Sainsbury's in Britain and Doug Tompkins' Esprit in the United States became keen to be associated with the new architecture. Esprit used, among others, Shiro Kuromata, Joe D'urso, Ettorre Sottsass and Norman Foster, while Sainsbury's caused some controversy with its choice of architects such as Nicholas Grimshaw, whose 'high tech' work many felt was not in keeping with food retailing. But, as Richard Rogers said, 'Modern architecture cannot be separated from modern life – it is part of life.'

In other fields of design the eighties demonstrated a vigorously eclectic, even at times confused, approach. Post-Modernists turned away from the stern functionalism of Bauhaus style and looked back towards the past with something of the same humanitarian concern as the earlier Arts and Crafts Movement. In turn, the 'New Design' movement, a reaction against Post-Modernism's recycling of past styles, rejected the past and instead explored a wide-ranging collage of ambiguous imagery gleaned from today's society, seeking to fuse the popular with the visionary.

RIGHT *Modern technology employed decoratively: Frosted Radio Light, by American artist Paul Seide, 1987. The intense colours are achieved by charging the spirals of glass with neon and mercury vapour from a transmitted radio field.*

LEFT *Amber Hiscott, one of the gifted stained-glass artists emerging in Britain today, produced this stained-glass canopy for Liberty & Co., London.*

LEFT *New materials include the refractory metals, whose potential for vivid colours has made them popular with jewellers. Anne Marie Shillitoe was one of the pioneers of their use in Britain, using them, unlike the majority of exponents, with subtlety in elegant curving forms such as this fibula in anodized titanium inlaid with tantalum and niobium.*

RIGHT *Glass chair by Danny Lane, 1980s; selected by the British Crafts Council as of exceptional merit. Lane, an American who has lived and worked in London since the mid-1970s, subverts conventional notions of how glass should be used. This chair, made of dozens of individual slices of float glass which are held together by rods in columns, is not very practical, being extremely heavy and not very comfortable, but it has a sculptural quality of which Gaudi or even Bugatti would have been proud.*

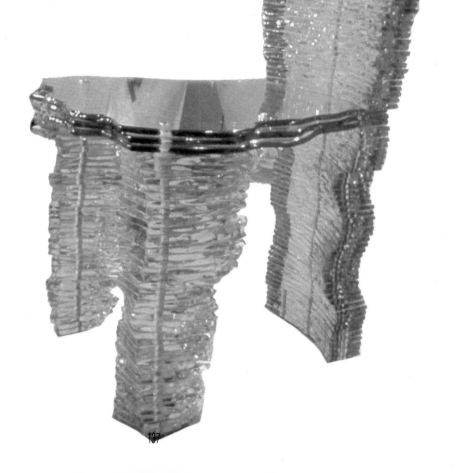

POST WAR DEVELOPMENTS

IND*ex*

ACKNOWLEDGEMENTS

Architectural Association: pp48; 84/85b; 102; 104. Patricia Bayer/Galerie Moderne: pp41t; 45br; 55; 71t; 76. Keith Baker: p28. Banham Archive, Berlin: p93b. Bauhaus Archive, Berlin: p97. Birmingham Museum and Art Gallery: p19b, Bridgeman Art Gallery: pp29; 31 (Bethnal Green Museum); 45bl. Emmet Bright: p34r. British Library: p40. Christies: pp33tl; 35 r; 42t; 47b; 48; 58t; 58l; 75b; 77; 82; 68b; 73t. Corning Museum of Glass: pp24; 56l. G Dagli Ortie: p55b. De Lorenzo, NY; p64br. Design Council: pp20; 100bl; 132. Alastair Duncan (photo Randy Jester): 99b. ET Archive: pp12to; 17; 23b; 47tr; 72bl; 81t. Philippe Garner: p38b. John Jesse and Irina Leski: p68. Lewis Gift (photo K Wetzel): p75t. Angelo Hornak: pp16t; 47t; 62; 78t; 81b; 105; 111b. AF Kersting: pp13bl; 16b; 18; 25l. Macdonald/Aldus Archive: p27b. Musee des Arts Decoratifs: pp71cl; 72r. Musee de l'Ecole de Nancy: p50. Robert Opie: p71br. Philips, London: p21. Riba (photo Geremy Butler) pp25r; 27r. Anne Marie Shilitoe: p136t. Sotheby's: pp10; 41b; 48; 57; 61; 106; 110. Ed Teitelman: pp90; 93t. Noel Tovey (photo Eileen Tweedy): pp4. Trevor Wood: pp39; 52b; 53. John Wyand: 52t.